The Gospel According to Job

Jerry McRaven

Jerry McRaven

The Gospel According to Job
Copyright © 2015 Jerry McRaven

All rights reserved. No part of this book may be used or reproduced by any means, graphic, electronic, or mechanical, including photocopying, recording, taping or by any information storage retrieval system without the written permission of the publisher except in the case of brief quotations embodied in critical articles and reviews. Because of the dynamic nature of the Internet, any web addresses or links contained in this book may have changed since publication and may no longer be valid. The views expressed in this work are solely those of the author and do not necessarily reflect the views of the publisher, and the publisher hereby disclaims any responsibility for them.

To contact the author Jerry "Mac" McRaven by email:
jerrymcraven@yahoo.com

ISBN# 978-1-60208-367-7

All Scripture quotations are taken from the: King James Version of the Holy Bible.

Cover Design: Linda K. Milam, FBC Publications and Printing
Editing and Interior Design: CBM Christian Book Editing
www.christian-book-marketing.com

Printed in the USA by
FBC Publications & Printing
Fort Pierce, FL 34982
www.fbcpublications.com

FOREWORD

BY

DR. JOE VANKOEVERING

It's a joy to meet and then get to know people who have been touched and impacted by the ministry, which God has called one to. For me, it's always been a wonderful benefit "to the job," relationships!

But on rare and special occasions, the Lord will "out do" Himself...and send someone into your life who will eventually become more than a partner or even a good friend. God is able to surprise you with one of those unique relationships . . . I think of David and Jonathan whose connection became "covenant!"

Well, Jerry McRaven and his precious wife, Janice are just such a couple to me...a covenant friendship. Deeper than friends and far deeper than merely partners, God Himself sent this special and unique couple into my life to bless, encourage and strengthen me.

Through this book you now have, "The Gospel According to Job" and my friend Jerry McRaven will give you a greater understanding of this mysterious Bible figure...Job, than you've ever had before. You will discover the power of the gospel

Jerry McRaven

"hidden" within the pages of the oldest book of the Bible. And lastly, Jerry will give you, through this book, that which he has given me many times…blessing, encouragement and strength!

It's time to "enjoy"…the Book of Job!

Dr. Joe VanKoevering
God's News Behind the News – President & Host
Gateway Christian Center – Senior Pastor

CONTENTS

Foreword by Dr. Joe VanKoevering   *iii*

Chapter One	From Sermon to a Book	7
Chapter Two	Searching for the Common Thread	23
Chapter Three	Beginning the Journey	35
Chapter Four	Introduction to the Hedge	49
Chapter Five	The Proto-Evangelium	63
Chapter Six	The Power of the Blood	75
Chapter Seven	Creation of the Hedge	87
Chapter Eight	Two Important Points	99
Chapter Nine	The Daily Sacrifice	111
Chapter Ten	Loss of the Hedge	119
Chapter Eleven	The Woven Thread	129
Chapter Twelve	The Final Conclusion	143
Epilogue		153
About the Author		155
Bibliography		157

Chapter One

From Sermon to a Book

I don't really know where to start, other than to say I am giving in to the pressure. Last night I concluded a four-day revival with my very good and longtime friend, Pastor Monty Roark of Parkton Assembly near Barnhart, Missouri. The concluding service to the revival was very moving and Brother Monty instructed me that I needed to write a book on my sermon which I had just preached entitled: "How The System Works."

I had been urged on a number of occasions, by different people from many churches, to write a book about the sermon, and often people would request a copy of my sermon notes. I am often asked if I have the message on tape or a disc. However, it wasn't until my dear friend, Monty, told me that the subject matter of my sermon needed to be in a book and given to the Body of Christ, that I began to actually entertain the thought of writing a book. I simply have not had a reason to write a book, nor have I had any desire to write. Besides, who would want to read a book written by me anyhow?

Being an author is simply something I have never aspired to be. The idea is totally adverse to my self-image, and foreign to my personality type. It just so happens that no matter where I travel to minister, (I am a full-time evangelist), if I preach the message: "How The System Works," church folks, and congregations all want to buy the book! It seems they all ask for the book. They all ask the question: "Why haven't you written a book?" I then must explain that I am not an author, and I have never written a book and I don't have time to write one anyway.

Let me clarify this one point, I certainly don't preach this message everywhere I go. I may preach it every year or two when God places the message on my heart, or I just feel the urge to preach it. I have even had pastors request that I preach it as they have been told about the sermon by other ministers. As an evangelist, I have never been one to just concentrate on this one message.

I will say though, that when God gave me this message, I knew even then that there was something special about it, and that it was not just your "typical" evangelistic sermon. I remember "how" God gave me the message, and that I was enthralled and engrossed in it for weeks and months. It had many layers and layers that came with it, and I now have condensed it and tried to make it fit into a typical and suitable time frame that the congregations can endure. I have tried to retain the most relevant concepts of the message without making it too lengthy.

It just so happens that two and a half weeks back from this writing, I attended a Prophecy Conference at Evangel World Prayer Center, which was hosted by Dr. Joe VanKoevering of God's News Behind the News. Evangel World Prayer Center is of course pastored by Brother Bob Rodgers and is located in Louisville, Kentucky. Pastor Rodgers treated us very cordially and we so much enjoyed the fellowship with him and the speakers. I reminded Brother Bob that when I was at Evangel World Prayer Center at the last prophecy conference, I mentioned to him I had one of his books that I really enjoyed. Brother Bob told me if I would bring the book with me next time, he would sign it. Well, guess what, I reminded him about that conversation from 6 years previous and Brother Rodgers said, "You know, I remember that." Then he proceeded and graciously signed my book for me.

It was during this conference that Pastor Jonathan Cahn was speaking and he mentioned the circumstances surrounding the authorship of his awesome and award winning book: "The Harbinger," that I came to remember what he had said about it. He mentioned that he also had never previously written a book and he then gave us an account of how God arranged miracle after miracle, and eventually caused the book to be published.

I spoke with Jonathan for a short while, I bought several books from his product table, and I informed him that I had now been present with him at some of his speaking engagements in at least five states. Jonathan simply smiled, shook my hand, and told me he appreciated my support. A short time later my wife, Janice, bought a few more of Jonathan's books as she identified herself to him. He then pointed to me as he thanked her and was quite gracious.

All of this seemed to come back to me as Brother Monty encouraged me to write something concerning the message: "How the System Works." People tell me that there is a revelation in the message, and quite frankly, I agree with them. I know that about fifteen years ago, my spirit was ablaze with what God had given me, which eventually turned out to be the message of, "How the System Works."

It seems that the message was "downloaded" into my spirit all at once. It was not a learning process, nor was it a system of discoveries, as most sermons seem to develop. It was a download. Immediately, I understood the message from beginning to end. I don't remember anything like this ever happening before. I felt my mind would explode with all that I was receiving.

Back then (about fifteen years ago,) I had probably read the Book of Job thirty or more times, but I had never seen this or heard anyone else preaching this specific material from the book. "How the System Works," is centered within the first chapter of the Book of Job. As you will see, the Bible itself is replete with references to chapter one, as this is where the message comes from.

Again, I never knew all this information was in Job chapter one, nor did I ever know of anyone else preaching about the first chapter of Job in such a way as I was seeing it now for the first time. I will admit that while I was attempting to absorb the download God had given me about Job chapter one, I did hear one person on television address a few of the aspects of the message. I was watching Christian television and I heard Pastor Jentezen Franklin of the Free Chapel Worship Center in Gainesville, Georgia, speaking in an interview where he mentioned something from Job chapter one that God had just given to me.

I was so impressed that someone of the stature of Jentezen Franklin saw the same thing God had just given to me, that I could hardly contain myself. As a result, I sent Brother Franklin an offering along with a letter, which probably seemed to him at the time as somewhat irrational, but sincere.

Nevertheless, I thanked him for his ministry and tried to explain what God had been showing me about Job, and how Jentezen himself had helped confirm to me that what I had received was from God.

I had hoped that Jentezen might respond to my attempt at a communication, but apparently, Brother Franklin's degree of discernment prohibited him from any attempt to make contact with me at that time. I have never made any further attempted communications with Brother Jentezen. As I look back now, not for any specific reason I can think of however, but all the same, it probably was not the right time in my life to be introduced to Brother Franklin. To this day, I continue to hold Jentezen Franklin in a very high regard, and he was an inspiration and encouragement to me, whether he knows it or not, when I saw him mention Job that night on television.

Besides this single instance with Jentezen Franklin, I never have heard anyone even remotely come close to even "skirt" or hint around the borders of the message of "How the System Works." However, for reasons I will detail later, the message has forever changed my life.

I would be doing God a great disservice if I didn't give Him credit for the entirety of the message. It also is for this reason that the message is "life changing." The response I get from preaching this one message is like no other sermon I have ever preached. We ministers have our "favorite" sermons that we like to preach. However, it doesn't seem to matter what I preach or what a sermon may be about, when I preach, "How The System Works," I always get a response from the people that it was life changing. I remember my Brother, Evangelist Ronnie Dean McRaven, telling me many years ago that he had preached: "Have The Gates of Death Been Opened Unto Thee," and "Who Is This Son Of Man?" over one-hundred times each. I also have to admit I have heard him preach each of those messages, and they truly are awesome.

As it pertains to sermons, as far as my ministry is concerned, it seems that whenever I preach, "How The System Works," I get "pumped" just knowing that "I" will be hearing it again. Not only am I excited to be preaching it, I still enjoy hearing it. It never fails to encourage me.

The Gospel According to Job

It was when I was attending a Prophecy Conference hosted by God's News Behind The News in Louisville, Ky., again at Pastor Bob Rodger's church, I first discussed this message with Dr. Joe Vankoevering of God's News, and Pastor of Gateway Christian Center in St. Petersburg, Florida. I believe the year was 2008, and I was talking to "Joe" about this message and I described just a small portion to him. Brother Joe seemed to be interested and even slightly intrigued with the prospects I had shared with him. Joe then told me, "Brother Mac, next time you preach this message, send me a copy; I would like to hear it." Janice and I just enjoyed the rest of the conference, and didn't think much more about it.

Speaking of this conference, I can't help but bring to your attention that three of the speakers at that conference have passed on to their heavenly rewards. This would include Dr. Hilton Sutton, Yaakov Rambsel and the late Brother Grant Jeffrey. As far as I am concerned, all three are irreplaceable. I would say that of the three, I was best acquainted with Grant Jeffrey. He was a real gentleman and Bible scholar. We had some very stimulating discussions and I have learned so much from him. I truly miss him, and prophecy conferences are not the same without him either, as we do not have anyone yet to take his place. His books were always something to be excited about.

I remember when I first met Grant (about fourteen years earlier) I had brought with me about twelve to fifteen of his books. I asked him if he would sign them for me and he said he would "gladly" sign them. I watched Grant as he signed all the books, which stacked about fourteen to eighteen inches high. He was a true man of God.

Years later, I saw Grant at a conference and I asked him this question: "Grant, have you ever thought of writing a book about a (government behind the government, or a shadow government) if you will?" Grant looked at his wife Kaye, then after about half a minute or so, Grant looked at me with a slight grin and said: "Shadow Government" is the title of my next book which I am now writing. We just looked at each other and could hardly believe what had just happened. I always felt kind of special when Grant would sometimes call me behind his product table to speak with me, and Kaye was always so friendly and gracious. My friend Jeff Harbuck who always worked Grant's product table, told me at a recent prophecy conference that "Grant liked you," which only added to my admiration of him.

I can also remember Grant joking with me on occasion and say something like, "How many books did you bring for me to sign this time?" I might then make a reply something like this: "I don't know, how many did you write?" To this day, I have never read a better book on Bible prophecy than Grant's book: "Armageddon: Appointment with Destiny." I told that to Grant on numerous occasions and he quipped with a smile: "Yes, but you know that you have set the bar pretty high!"

I guess by now, you have surmised that I am a person who is what you might call a Bible prophecy enthusiast. I love Bible prophecy, and I enjoy hearing someone expound upon it, especially someone who has done their research and is a true Bible believer.

I came by this trait honestly, as my Uncles' Tom and Dean Heady Jr. were my mentors in the early stages of my Bible prophecy teaching. Both have passed on now, but they were great men of God with a very discerning aptitude for Bible prophecy.

Upon my mother's divorce from my father when I was age eight or nine, I was fortunate enough and blessed of God to be raised with my grandparents. It just so happened that Tom and Dean at the time still lived with my grandparents as Tom was fourteen years older than myself and Dean was about sixteen years my elder.

My grandfather, Dean Heady Senior, pastored the Berryman Assembly of God Church. Everybody in the country always said he was, I quote, "The best preacher I had ever heard." Of course, the same was said about his brother, my great uncle, Floyd E. Heady. Between the two, you would hear some of the greatest preaching you could possibly be exposed to.

This tradition continued through Tom and Dean Jr., as they were known as the "Heady Brothers" Evangelistic Team. I have seen Dean Jr. preach for ten to fifteen minutes at a time and do nothing at all but quote scriptures. The video screen operators in churches always said they could "never keep up with Dean" with putting the scriptures on screen as he could quote them faster than they could put them up. Man, do I miss these guys! They were real men of God; they lived the life, and they set an exemplary life pattern for me to emulate.

Even now, I can hardly go anywhere that someone doesn't remind me they received Christ under Tom, Dean, Dean Sr., or my Great Uncle Floyd's ministries. They also say these were the best preachers they ever heard, and it is true, they were some of the most powerful preachers I have ever witnessed.

My Brother Ronnie also is often referenced as: "Ronnie Dean, The Preachin' Machine." If I was just half the preacher as any of these founding family ministers, I could feel secure that I had made a lasting impact upon the Body of Christ. It is an honor to just be mentioned in the same breath as them. I could go on and on and tell you of these and other family ministers, and of the many miracles that took place in their lives, but that is a story for another book.

To me, Bible prophecy is one of the best vehicles there is to bring someone into an honest and profound interest of Scripture. Since Scripture is about one-third Bible prophecy, you have a way to describe current events to someone in light of the Bible. Bible prophecy serves as a unique way to introduce people to the Bible and its teachings. This concept has become extremely evident with the exponential advent of the Bible prophecy stage being set and observed in today's world.

You simply cannot turn on your TV for a few minutes without someone mentioning Israel or Jerusalem, Syria, Iraq, Iran, Turkey, Jordan, Saudi Arabia, or Egypt, etc. etc., all of which are featured in End Times Bible prophecy. I am convinced we are living in the last of the Last Days.

The more I study, the more I am convinced that it was the Bible that had the answers all along. The same holds true for today, as in Daniel's time. Daniel asked the question of Nebuchadnezzar: (paraphrasing), "Couldn't the Astrologers, the Soothsayers, the Chaldeans, or Stargazers give the king the answers he requests?" Daniel went on to say: "But there is a God in Heaven who can show the king what is troubling him."

As you can probably surmise by now, I am a big fan of Dr. Joe VanKoevering. At this writing, I have attended no less than seventeen or eighteen of the International Prophecy Conferences hosted by Pastor Joe. I have attended numerous Prophecy Summits and events hosted by: "Prophecy in the News," Future Congress with Tom Horn and Gary Stearman, Worldview Weekend with Brannon Howse, and others, (of which I have thoroughly enjoyed them all), but Joe is the absolute best conference host there is.

It was around 2010 when I next preached: "How the System Works." I preached this message locally in Farmington, Missouri at the Abundant Life Church pastored by my longtime friend and "one of my favorite preachers," Pastor Rick Hensley. By this time, it had been about two years since my conversation with Joe VanKoevering about the message, which we had previously discussed in Louisville.

Brother Hensley gave me a few copies of the message after church. The next time I attended Brother Hensley's church, I was told that there had been one or two people in the church that had been healed of chronic conditions as they simply remembered what I had preached in the message as I had related what had happened to me.

In the message I explain that I had been healed of Restless Leg Syndrome and Chronic Headaches of which I had suffered for decades. I suffered from restless leg for more than twenty years and from headaches for more than forty years. I am now sixty-three and I haven't had a headache or an episode of Restless Leg Syndrome since the very night I was given the "download" of this message from God about fifteen years ago. That's a fact. I don't know how the restless leg became a part of my life, but the headaches were a result of a sports accident I suffered when I was young as I collided heads with another baseball player as we were both attempting to catch the same fly ball. The doctor told me I would have severe headaches as a result for the rest of my life, and he was right. As another by-product of the accident, I also developed a small tumor that had to be frozen and then burned off from just above my left eye.

Anyhow, I remembered my conversation with Dr. Joe VanKoevering and I sent him a copy of the message I had preached at Brother Rick Hensley's. I had no idea if Joe would remember our conversation or not, nor did I know if he would even listen to the CD.

To my surprise, I received a phone call from Pastor Joe at about seven o'clock a.m. (central standard time) about two weeks later. Dr. Joe said he had just listened to the CD while driving in his car. He said he briefly remembered the conversation, and was curious to hear the CD. Then he said these words to me: "Brother Mac, when you come down for the next prophecy conference, come a little early and preach that message for me in my church." He then told me that "God" had spoke to him to have me preach, "How the System Works" in Gateway Christian Center. I don't remember, but I know that it was in the spring (March or April) of 2011 when Pastor Joe called me, and the date for the engagement in his church would be in February of 2012.

I remember as I presented Pastor Joe with a 2011 baseball World Series Champions St. Louis Cardinals ball cap. I did this as I knew Joe to be a St. Louis Cardinals fan as they used to practice during spring training in St. Petersburg Fl., the home of Dr. Joe. As a boy, Joe would watch the Cardinals play and he became a fan.

I went to Gateway Christian Center and preached, "How the System Works," for Pastor Joe on Feb. 26th 2012. We had a great service, and people from the church asked me if I had a book, or if I was going to write one about the message. I remember Pastor Joe telling me that the people loved the message, and that they liked me too.

I couldn't begin to explain just how humbling that was for me. This is because of all the prophecy conferences I attended in this church, and knowing of the caliber of Bible prophecy experts and dignitaries that had spoken there, such as: Dr. Chuck Missler, Dr.. Ed Hindson, Grant Jeffrey, Dr.. Hilton Sutton, Dr. David Reagan, Dr. Tim Lahaye, Don Perkins, Bill Cloud, Gary Kah, Perry Stone, Jonathan Cahn, Avi Lipkin, Ray Brubaker, Dr.. Randall Price, and Mark Hitchcock just to name a few. Virtually the Who's Who of Bible prophecy have spoken here.

As far as I was concerned it was truly an honor to stand behind the sacred desk that so many of my prophecy heroes had stood behind. Not to mention Pastor Joe VanKoevering. I remember many times coming away from a prophecy conference and asking Janice, "What speaker did you enjoy most?" Oftentimes her answer agreed with mine, as it was, Joe VanKoevering. We continue to appeal to Pastor Joe to not sell himself short, as he often will yield his speaking time to another. But due to his unselfish spirit, Joe often continues to yield his allotted prophecy conference time to someone else.

In March of 2013 I preached, "How the System Works," again in Calhoun, Georgia for our dear friends, Pastors Roy and Martha Smith. The people there asked for my sermon notes, and wanted to know if I had any CD's of the message. It just so happened I had two copies of the message when I preached it at Gateway Christian Center for Brother Joe. This phenomenon continues to this day as people either want the notes, CD's, or a book.

Again, I must reiterate that the message is not mine; it was downloaded to me by the Holy Spirit. I can't, nor will I take any credit for it. I am just grateful that God saw fit to give me such a powerful message that is so life changing. When Brother Monty Roark urged me to write the book, he knew that people elsewhere had requested that I write one. He then told me that he not only seconded the request, but he third, fourth, fifth, sixth, and seventhed it.

I must admit that somehow I knew all along that God would lead me to write the book at some point in my life. No matter how much I tried to convince myself that I never had time to write a book, I instinctively knew that I would write it. I don't feel this urge about any other subject, but I somehow realized that it was inevitable. I guess it finally caught up with me. If it had been someone else besides Brother Monty, it probably wouldn't be happening. Brother Monty Roark is several years younger than myself, but I remember listening to him preach when he was in his middle to late teens! We have always supported each other, and I was conducting revivals with Brother Monty before Janice and I were married, some 35 years ago. Prior to our recent revival, I requested that he speak on Sunday morning because I wanted to hear him preach. I was not disappointed. His message about the Rapture of the church was so anointed and awe inspiring.

Jerry McRaven

Chapter Two

Searching for the Common Thread

You just don't hear preachers preach on the Rapture much anymore. Part of the reason is that a large portion of our churches and ministers don't believe in it these days. Sad. I can remember as a child growing up in the Assemblies of God Churches, that you could hardly hear any preacher in any given church service not make reference to it. Times have changed indeed. As you will see later, the Rapture is suggested in Job, chapter one.

Yes, times have changed. I am not going to go into the problems with today's churches, and there are many. Of course, I suppose such problems are relative or they are subject to interpretation. To some, a mega-church is something to be desired. To someone else a small congregation is more favorable. It makes no difference to me, which you attend or pastor as long as the people are being taught the truth of Scripture. I myself am what you would consider by today's standards to be conservatively Pentecostal.

This does not prevent me from ministering in other churches like Baptists or churches of similar beliefs, as I continue to speak in Baptist churches and thoroughly enjoy doing it. These people love God, they are my brothers in Christ, they are very warm and cordial to me personally, and they have a deep and abiding love for Bible prophecy. Many of my favorite prophecy teachers are Baptist ministers.

It has never been my intention or ambition to try to "pentecostalize" the Christians of these churches. Such is not even an issue, besides, with all the rampant error being espoused by the hyper charismatics these days, I don't want them to imagine that I am even remotely associated with that group, or practice what they do. At one time, I was considered in unity with the charismatic movement, but not now, as I don't like where it is going these days, as I have grave reservations about the entire movement.

I will just put it on the line. If you are from an Emergent Church persuasion, this book probably is not for you. If you are a die-hard extreme Word of Faith enthusiast, this probably will not be your cup of tea either. I doubt that the members of the New Apostolic Reformation will want to endorse it. I seriously doubt this book will reach the heights of the top ten best sellers list of the New Age Movement, Seeker Sensitive Churches, Kingdom Now, Chrislamic Devotees, or make the newest edition of the Elijah List.

I could continue citing such dissenters, but I do think it is possible that some serious churchgoers including Baptists, Methodists, Presbyterians, and Independents will find this book inspiring. As a matter of fact, I believe that any true born again believer will find this book rather refreshing. It is possible that some of the others will as well, but I'm not counting on it. As far as the Hebrew Roots Movement is concerned, I guess we will just have to wait and see.

I am not trying to start a spiritual confrontation with anyone or any movement or denomination. The truth is the truth, and I believe this message speaks the truth. As a minister of the gospel of Jesus Christ, I am required to preach the gospel. Sadly, in these times the Gospel may not be the most popular message out there. But then again, it never has been. Just try to calculate all the martyrs there have been throughout history for nothing more than just preaching the Gospel.

It just so happens that history shows us that all the above churches and organizations at one time believed in and taught in the "blood atonement" of Jesus Christ. Some still do, while others may make reference to it. But too many are preaching a different gospel altogether. There may even be some Catholics that find this book interesting. I certainly hope so, as I welcome everyone to read it.

The common denominator between all Christian based religious organizations whether Pentecostal or not, Protestant or Catholic, have a common thread. That thread is linked to Jesus

Christ and what He accomplished on the cross. What Christ did on the cross is profoundly unprecedented. It is the basis for all Christian thought. If you take away from Christianity the effects of the cross, you merely have just another religious system.

Yes, Christianity is unique, as religious systems are man's ways to find God. Christianity is God's introduction to man. We can actually communicate with God Himself, and we can read what He has to say to us. We can be in relationship with God. Because of this, I don't believe this relationship depends upon our use of Rosary Beads or how many "Hail Mary's" we say today, since that tends to encourage a "Works Based" system. In spite of what we see today, true Christianity is not intended to be a works based form of worship.

I recently heard Oprah Winfrey say something like this: "If you have a believing form of religion, you are not doing it right, what you need is a (feeling) form of worship and religion." Well, I know Oprah has many more members in her church than I can address in one book, but she is sadly mistaken. **John 3:18 says:** "He that believeth on him is not condemned: but he that believeth not is condemned already, because he hath not believed in the name of the only begotten Son of God."

I don't serve God by my feelings. Sometimes your feelings can be misdirected, or even mistaken. It is simply sad that so many people today agree with Oprah Winfrey and believe that you must experience some type of feeling to encounter God. I will not be afraid to admit that many times I do feel God's presence. And while we are in the presence of God, we can have certain feelings of awe, grace, repentance, energy, anointing, happiness, joy, or even feelings associated with burdens, intercession, or heaviness.

But, our relationship with God is not based upon these experiences. Our relationship with Jesus Christ is based upon what He did for us. I believe in what Jesus did! In John 9:35 the blind man Christ healed is cast out of the synagogue. Jesus confronts him and says in **John 9:35,** "Jesus heard that they had cast him out; and when he had found him, he said unto him, 'Dost thou believe on the Son of God?'"

This is what Christ wants from us. He wants us to believe in Him as the Son of God, and in what He did. After all, Jesus made it possible for us to be reconciled back to God the Father. Here we are, sinful creatures who can be reconciled back to a Holy God. How awesome is that?

The problem man has is that we are all sinful and have a sin nature. By a sin nature, we understand that no one had to teach us to lie, cheat, steal, envy, or lust. When your mother asked if you had eaten any of the icing from her chocolate cake, you said, "No!" But when she saw chocolate icing around your mouth, she knew what had happened. The illustration here is this; you lied to protect yourself, as it was in your nature to do so. You were not taught how to do this, you were not instructed to do this, it was just a natural part of being a fallen creature.

Some today teach that your sin nature is destroyed when you are born again. **Romans 7:24,** "O wretched man that I am! Who shall deliver me from the body of this death?" Someone needed to explain that to the Apostle Paul. Paul wrote much of the New Testament to instruct Christians how to have power over sin. In **John 8:34,** "Jesus answered them, 'Verily, verily, I say unto you, whosoever committeth sin is the servant of sin.'"

No, I don't like where I see the Body of Christ going these days. We have Word of Faith leaders and other charismatics meeting with Pope Francis, we have church denominations ordaining gay ministers and bishops, and we have entire church denominations that have boycotted Israeli products and travel to the Holy Land as they believe Israel is illegally occupying Judea and Samaria, or the West Bank.

We have leaders that believe the Jews living in Israel have no prophetic future whatsoever and that the church has replaced them. Replacement theology is common these days. Pope Francis is on record that he believes the Jews need to give up the West Bank and Judea to the Palestinians. This is what God says: **Joel 3:2,** "I will also gather all nations, and will bring them down into the valley of Jehoshaphat, and will plead with them there for my people and *for* my heritage Israel, whom they have scattered among the nations, and parted my land."

God says Israel is His land, and He does not want it parted or divided. He is speaking here about Armageddon, and He is angry that His land has been divided. As children of God, we need to be on the right side of what God wants. How can a church or a denomination be so far out of the will of God as to totally disenfranchise God's natural people? If my memory serves me correctly, Jesus Christ was Jewish and from the tribe of Judah. I personally bear no ill will against the Palestinian people, but there is no Palestinian history, no Palestinian language, culture, religion, land, historical sites, etc. Palestinians are Arabs from the surrounding countries of Israel who by in large practice Islam and its culture.

They are Palestinian simply by the fact they lived in the country of Israel or Palestine as it is called in the Muslim culture. The Palestinians already were given a land; it was called Jordan.

With all this going on, it amazes me what the Church seems to be involved with. When I think about the message of, "How the System Works," it brings me back to the basics of the Gospel. Today's churches seem to have lost their way somehow.

Since when has passing out bottled water become a "ministry?" Why do Christian leaders speak at the Islamic Society of North America? Why do Christian leaders join such groups as "interfaith" organizations? Why do some churches invite Muslim Clerics to speak, and show me a "gay" church anywhere in Scripture. Why is Chrislam flourishing, and why do our Christian Denominational leaders go to Brigham Young University and refer to the Mormon students there as Christians? The late prophet of the Mormon Church, Gordon B. Hinckley said and I quote: "In bearing testimony of Jesus Christ, President Hinckley spoke of those outside the church who say latter-day saints 'do not believe in the traditional Christ.' 'No, I don't. The traditional Christ of whom they speak is not the Christ of whom I speak. For the Christ of whom I speak has been revealed in this the dispensation of the fullness of times. He together with his father, appeared to the boy Joseph Smith in the year 1820, and when Joseph left the grove that day, he knew more of the nature of God than all the learned ministers of the gospel of the ages.'" (LDS church news week ending June 20, 1998, p. 7).

I am reminded what the Apostle Paul had to say about such goings on: **Ephesians 5:11,** "And have no fellowship with the unfruitful works of darkness, but rather reprove *them*." Somehow, I have the feeling that the Apostle Paul wouldn't go to such places. But if he did, I don't think he would call them brothers, I imagine he would preach Jesus Christ and Him crucified!

What has happened to the Church? It appears we have lost focus of what brought us here in the first place. I remember what it was that brought me to an altar. Some old-time Gospel preacher preached the message of Jesus Christ and Him crucified on the cross of Calvary where He shed His blood and died for me. The Church needs to get focused once again on "The Gospel!"

The problem with the true Gospel message to this present world, is that for some reason church leadership has come to the conclusion that not only do we need to change our methods, we by necessity, need to change our message! Today it seems that Christendom is embracing the Pope, Chrislam, The LGBT Community, Liberation and Black Liberation Theology, of which none are compatible with the pure Gospel of Jesus Christ. And if

Islam is such a peaceful religion, why are there so many refugees fleeing from Islamic countries? I see no refugees fleeing from predominantly Christian nations, but I do see refugees seeking asylum in them.

Well, I guess I have rode that horse long enough for one book. I am just trying to make a point. That point being: the focus of the Church is not Christ and Him crucified anymore, and the "blood of Christ" has become a non-issue.

This is where the message of "How the System Works," comes into play. For the purposes of this book, I have chosen to give the book a different title. Don't ask me why, but I feel strongly that the title should now be known as: "THE GOSPEL ACCORDING TO JOB." So, if you have purchased this book, you will now recognize the title. Although the book has a different title, the subject matter is to be taken directly from the sermon of "How the System Works" by Evangelist Jerry "Mac" McRaven.

Before I begin to develop the actual message itself, I want to make a simple observation. It seems to me that the Gospel presentation has changed since I was young. The emphasis today seems to be on personal wealth, being happy, enjoying our lives to the fullest, building church memberships, providing church atmospheres that the public is comfortable with, and personal empowerment concepts. While many of these ideas may be motivational, I do not perceive any of them to be part of the Gospel, with the exception of being happy and enjoying life, as a true Christian will experience both without having to work at it.

You would be hard-pressed to find Jesus Christ teaching on becoming wealthy or providing an atmosphere that is conducive to make sinners feel comfortable. It was Jesus who called the religious people of his day "hypocrites." (Obviously not the most popular of messages), then Christ would heal someone and have the audacity to tell them: "Go and sin no more." (another unpopular theme.) People today don't like being told they are a sinner. The truth is the truth however, and Jesus always told the truth regardless of its popularity. It just seems to me that many of today's churches have abandoned the truth for a message somewhere between "you are a God," and "the Israelites are Christ killers."

So, without further adieu, let us now go into the actual message itself and see what all the "hub-ub" is about. I don't have a specific text for the message, I simply start with Job chapter 1, verse 1. While you are tempted to go to Job and see it for yourself, allow me to explain to you what I told Dr. Joe VanKoevering during our initial discussion in 2008.

I stated that I believed Job was most likely the oldest book of Scripture and that from the very first page of Scripture, the Gospel was proclaimed. I believed that the keys to salvation, healing, and deliverance were in evidence right there on the pages of Job chapter 1. I also believe that the pure simplicity of the Gospel is demonstrated from the very first page of the Bible, as it is believed the Book of Job was "written" prior to any of the other books of the Bible.

And why wouldn't God begin His Word with the Gospel itself? After all, Jesus is: the "Alpha and the Omega," the First and the Last, the Beginning and the End. Thusly, we have "The Gospel According to Job."

When speaking of "How the System Works," we must take note of the fact that God does have a system. If we are to be successful in our relationship with our Heavenly Father, we need to be sure that we are not operating outside of His prescribed system. With this in mind, it is necessary to be acquainted with God's system and to know for a surety if we are in compliance with it or not. As long as we are within the rules of the system, it will work for us, but anytime we are outside of it, we can't expect God to continue to bless and protect us.

Satan himself has a system as well, but since God is sovereign and in power as being omnipotent, Satan is forced to work within the confines of the system God has set up. We must understand each system in order to function effectively as Christians at full capacity. Anything less than full capacity could result in disaster. Just look at Samson for example. He understood how things worked, but he ignored certain aspects of his Nazarite vows to his own destruction.

Jerry McRaven

Chapter Three

Beginning the Journey

So let us now begin the journey into:

"The Gospel According to Job"

Job 1:1, "There was a man in the land of Uz, whose name was Job; and that man was perfect and upright, and one that feared God, and eschewed evil."

These are simply statements of fact about a real person named Job. Job is not a mythical character, as many so-called Bible scholars today falsely claim. Today, it has become the popular theme to say that the Book of Job is merely a book of poetry with mythical characters. For me, it is quite difficult to imagine God placing in His Biblical canon a book about someone with the testimony of Job and it not be real. After all, if the book is just mythical and not real, why should anyone take it seriously? What lesson is there to be learned from just a simple mythical story?

However, if the book of Job is God's Word, it is as powerful as any other portion of God's Word. This being true, since the lessons learned in Job are actual occurrences, when a person uses the book as an example, the lessons learned can be repeated successfully. Such is not always the case with a fable or myth. I agree that Job is poetic, but I beg to differ about it simply being a mythical book, as the book itself has come under attack by many of today's so-called Bible scholars.

Let's go to Scripture and look for some facts. Abraham begat Isaac and Isaac begat Esau and Jacob. Esau had 5 sons, and Jacob had 12 sons. This we know from the Bible itself. There is no question as to these facts. In Genesis 36:10 Esau's firstborn son is identified as Eliphaz, while Genesis 36:18 identifies that Jacob's 5th son was named Issachar. Again, these facts are not in question.

Genesis 46:13, "And the sons of Issachar; Tola, and Phuvah, and Job, and Shimron."

1 Chronicles 7:1 says it this way: Now the sons of Issachar *were*, Tola, and Puah, Jashub, and Shimron, four."

You will immediately notice that there are different spellings here. Phuvah has become Puah. This shouldn't be any cause for alarm. And Job has now become Jashub. I would not think this to be any cause for alarm either. We already know that such names as Eleazar can be simplified into "Lazarus." I could give other examples also, but I knew an old gentlemen when I was growing up named, Jasper. Jasper was known to everyone as "Jap." It is easy to understand that Jashub would be simplified to Job. In any event, only the spellings are different; they obviously are the same persons. We must also take into consideration that the Book of Genesis refers to the man named, Job. Genesis would chronologically have been the 2nd book of the Bible actually written. This gives more credence to the first mentioned spelling of his name.

Let's investigate a little further. In Job chapter 2 when Job's so-called comforters came to comfort him, Eliphaz the Temanite was not only Job's friend, they were 2nd cousins. Eliphaz being the direct son of Esau. Eliphaz would have been first cousin to Issachar, Job's father. This would have made Eliphaz and Job 2nd cousins.

We know this to be a fact since this Eliphaz was known as the "Temanite." Well, Eliphaz came from a place known as Teman. It is also a fact that Teman was the name of the firstborn son of Eliphaz. These are real people that can be found in Scripture. As it turns out, Jacob himself was Job's grandfather, being the father of Issachar.

Now, let's go back to Job 1:1 for some clarification. **Job 1:1,** "There was a man in the land of Uz, whose name *was* Job; and that man was perfect and upright, and one that feared God, and eschewed evil."

First of all, we know there was a land of Uz as it is mentioned in Jeremiah 25:20, and in Lamentations 4:21. As Job begins, it mentions that Job himself lived in the land of Uz. According to this verse, Job was perfect and upright, he feared God, and eschewed evil.

To eschew evil means quite distinctly to deliberately avoid or abstain from the very presence of evil. A pretty good trait to have I might say. We would do good to follow Job's example in that regard. Job was upright and feared God which means he obeyed God and reverenced Him. However, there is that awkward and disturbing word; "Perfect."

How could Job be perfect? This is an impossibility isn't it? We know that there have been no perfect human beings, with one exception. That exception being Jesus Christ Himself. Besides, remember this verse? **Romans 3:23,** "For all have sinned, and come short of the glory of God; . . ." Since we know this verse to be true, then just how can Job be perfect? We know that all men have sinned and are in need of a savior. This is a fact, and this also includes Job.

As a result, we must conclude that Job was a moral man who worshipped and feared God, but was not without sin or sinless. Therefore, we must understand Job's perfection was not that he was sinless, but perfect in a spiritual way. This is summed up by the conclusion that Job was "perfect" not as a man without sin, but "perfect" in his approach to serving God, and being perfect in his approach to serving God is the key to his blessings and protection.

I would submit to you, that if we were perfect in our approach to serving God, as Job was, God would be more real in our lives. I

The Gospel According to Job

also believe we would understand the nature of God more clearly under such circumstances, making it easier to serve Him. We would not be in doubt quite so often as to try to "find the will of God."

Job 1:5, "And it was so, when the days of *their* feasting were gone about, that Job sent and sanctified them, and rose up early in the morning, and offered burnt offerings *according* to the number of them all: for Job said, it may be that my sons have sinned, and cursed God in their hearts. Thus did Job continually."

As far as Job was concerned, if there was any sins committed, by any of his family members, it was to be atoned for immediately. Job did not beat around the proverbial bush, he would proceed immediately to prepare a blood sacrifice for any sins of his family or himself. Job did not waste any time in preparing a sacrifice.

It also must be noted that not just any old sacrifice would do. Job always prepared a "blood sacrifice." Verse 5 is very plain that the sacrifices of Job were burnt offerings. This means an animal was sacrificed and it was a sacrifice of blood. Job was convinced that sin must be covered by a blood atonement.

Job 1:6, "Now there was a day when the sons of God came to present themselves before the Lord, and Satan came also among them."

This is a very interesting verse. I understand that these things occurred prior to Jesus going to the cross. I also realize that the protocols may have changed somewhat after Jesus returned to heaven to be seated at the right hand of the throne of God. But then

39

again, they may not have. I do know that Satan is still the "Accuser of the Brethren," and the Book of Job is a perfect example of how Satan earned that title.

The picture here is that all of God's created angels were summoned to give an account to God of their whereabouts and activities. Even Satan was obligated to make an appearance. Such an event must have been quite spectacular with all of the angel hierarchy passing before God in full review.

The angels were to give an account of their time and actions to God. Satan is not allowed to operate outside of the parameters of the system God has set up. God has a system, and Satan is confined to function within the framework of that system. Satan has no authority to deviate from what he is allowed to do. Remember in the Book of Jude:

Jude 1:9, "Yet Michael the archangel, when contending with the Devil he disputed about the body of Moses, durst not bring against him a railing accusation, but said, the Lord rebuke thee."

Satan understood by Michael that he was being rebuked by the Lord and not by Michael. Since Satan knows his limitations, he did not register any more complaints or accusations and accepted things as they were and did not pursue the matter.

Job 1:7, "And the Lord said unto Satan, whence comest thou? Then Satan answered the Lord, and said, from going to and fro in the earth, and from walking up and down in it." Here, God specifically asked Satan where he had been and what he had been doing. Satan was required to give an account of himself as well as the other angels that were summoned.

In verse 7, Satan explained he had been walking to and fro in the Earth. This explains first and foremost, that this natural Earth is under constant surveillance by the spirit world. What Satan was doing here seems to be a common practice. It appears that angels of all persuasions are commonly patrolling the Earth realm.

Zechariah 1:9-11, "Then said I, 'O my Lord, what *are* these?' And the angel that talked with me said unto me, 'I will shew thee what these *be*.' **10** And the man that stood among the myrtle trees answered and said, 'These *are they* whom the Lord hath sent to walk to and fro through the earth.' **11** And they answered the angel of the Lord that stood among the myrtle trees, and said, 'We have walked to and fro through the earth, and, behold, all the earth sitteth still, and is at rest.' "

It is here that we need to take a moment to investigate what is being said. Oftentimes we tend to forget that we are spiritual beings ourselves, and that we have been plunged into a world that is populated with other spirits that we cannot see.

The reason we can't see into the spirit world is due to the fact our spirits are enclosed inside "vessels of clay." We are spirit beings within a human body. Once our body has expired, our spirits are released from it. Once this happens we can immediately see into the spirit world as it was our bodies themselves that prohibited us from seeing into the spiritual realm.

One example in Scripture where someone is allowed to see into the spiritual realm that previously could not, is found in: **2 Kings 6:17,** "And Elisha prayed, and said, 'Lord, I pray thee, open his eyes, that he may see.' And the Lord opened the eyes of the young man; and he saw: and, behold, the mountain *was* full of horses and chariots of fire round about Elisha."

If our spirits could exit outside our bodies, we would see the spirits all around us and everywhere we would go. We would not only see the godly angels, we would also see all the demonic forces around us. We simply often forget that there is a constant war being waged all around us between good and evil.

This spiritual war never stops, and there are battles being won and lost every second. It just so happens that we can't see all of the activity that is going on, but that does not mean the battles are not happening simply because we don't see it with our eyes. Elisha the prophet could see into this realm, and his servant did also after God opened his eyes.

We as people of God have angels encamped about us as the Bible says. **Psalms 34:7,** "The angel of the Lord encampeth round about them that fear him, and delivereth them." But these angels are not instructed to "restrain us" in any way from our human emotions or to try to persuade us or prevent us from acting in a specific way or to not do as "our will" might dictate. We are free moral agents to do as we please, whether our decision is the right thing to do, or whether it is not. God gives us such free moral agency, which in effect, gives us total control of our actions and thoughts. These heaven sent angels are present around us to protect us from any undue temptations or unlawful trickery that Satan might try to get away with. Satan surely is capable of creating extenuating circumstances where he can apply "grey area" styled calisthenics to try to circumvent God's system of jurisprudence. Plainly stated, Satan doesn't play fair.

This is evidenced by the words of Eve after she tasted of the forbidden fruit and she exclaimed in: **Genesis 3:13**, "And the Lord God said unto the woman, 'What *is* this *that* thou hast done?' And the woman said, 'The serpent beguiled me, and I did eat.' "

Eve is basically explaining to God that the serpent lied to her and beguiled her. She was stating that he didn't treat me fairly. He used guile, from where we get our word "guilty."

Sadly, it is often overlooked by many of us that we do live in a world that is populated by both good and evil spirits. Each of these spirit groups encounter each other when we are tempted. The angel is present, and so is the evil spirit.

An evil spirit will initiate a thought into your mind even as the angel observes. It is your reaction to the demonic suggestion that the evil spirit is waiting to see. If you obviously are not "taking the bait," the evil spirit may leave you alone, or suggest something else. If you are weak and succumb to the demonic temptation, the angel is helpless to do anything since you are a free moral agent and he will not interfere.

On the other hand, if you refuse to listen to the temptation and you begin to pray for strength, or to call upon God, the angel is then empowered by your actions. The angel now has authority to remove the evil spirit from you and guard you from any further attacks he might try. In this battle, God wins. But tomorrow is another day filled with more temptations. Satan will keep after you until he finds an area he feels might bring him success. This does however explain what James meant when he said in: **James 4:7,** "Submit yourselves therefore to God. Resist the devil, and he will flee from you." I would venture to say that these demons would rather flee than to have to deal with the angels that have charge over you. We simply can't forget how these battles are won and lost.

We are probably surrounded by angels and evil spirits at any given time. I don't know to what extent, but we know the battle is raging. There is nothing we do that is ever totally in secret. If we could only see into the spirit world, we would be aware of this. At the Great White Throne Judgment, there will be nothing hidden from God that will not be disclosed or declared.

It is quite possible that Satan was patrolling the Earth when he confronted Eve. Satan must have already become a fallen creature at this point as he surely demonstrated he was not in harmony with God by tempting Eve as he did. This episode does explain what Satan does however, when he is on patrol of the Earth. He observes.

Revelation 12:10 speaks of Satan as the Accuser of the Brethren. In order for Satan to accuse you, he must be aware of what you did as he needs something to accuse you of. Somehow I have the belief that Satan knows what you did because he "instigated" the original temptation, and as a result of this he or one of his emissaries was actually present to observe your indiscretion. We notice that Satan was not rebuked by God when he mentioned to him that he was walking to and fro through the Earth. Apparently Satan and godly angels regularly patrol the Earth realm.

In Job 1:8 it says, "And the Lord said unto Satan, 'Hast thou considered my servant Job, that there is none like Him in the earth, a perfect and an upright man, one that feareth God, and escheweth evil?' Here, God is asking Satan if he has encountered Job during his observation patrols on the Earth. As you will see later, the word "considered" used here will become more revealing.

It has always amazed me when God asks a question. Remember what God said to Cain: **Genesis 4:9-10,** "And the Lord said unto Cain, 'Where *is* Abel thy brother?' And he said, 'I know not: *Am* I my brother's keeper?' **10** And he said, 'What hast thou done? The voice of thy brother's blood crieth unto me from the ground.' When God asked Cain where Abel was, He knew the answer already. It is the same here. God knew perfectly well that Satan had encountered Job during his observations and patrols of the Earth.

God knew because He was aware of the battles that had taken place with Job. We are never tempted that God doesn't know about it rather quickly as the angels assigned to us have a direct spirit connection to God. So, when God asked Satan if he had considered his servant Job, God wanted to know from Satan why he was not successful in his temptations of Job. God wanted to hear Satan's side of the story.

One thing here I think is quite significant. God and Satan both knew Job on a first name basis! That is rather incredible when you think about it. I certainly would wish that I could be so notable. Satan did not have to ask God: "Job who?"

Verse 8 here gives us some very pertinent information that we need to review. By asking Satan if he had considered His servant Job, God was actually asking:

Have you challenged Job?

Have you taken heed to Job?

Have you investigated Job's will and intellect?

Have you closely observed Job?

In Job 1:8, God tells Satan that there is not a man on Earth like Job. Now that's quite a statement, isn't it? God understands Job to be one of a kind. And as a result, God wants Satan to give him an assessment of Job from Satan's perspective.

Somehow I feel that God was aware of Satan's frustration when it pertained to Job. God understood all the aspects of Satan's attempts against Job, but He wanted to hear Satan try to excuse himself for his lack of success and inability to penetrate Job's seeming ability to remain upright before God.

This brings us again to verse 7 where God tells Satan that there is "none" like Job in the Earth! God knows that Job is unique in all the Earth and there are none else like Him. This accounts for

The Gospel According to Job

Satan's ineffectual means to win against Job. God reminds Satan that Job is "perfect" and upright. Job is one that fears God and eschews evil.

Job 1:9, "Then Satan answered the Lord, and said, 'Doth Job fear God for nought?' " Now we are going to hear Satan's side of the story. This is what God was seeking from Satan all along. It begins with Satan explaining to God that what Job is doing for him through his life of obedience and worship approach, is basically due to what God is doing for Job. After all, Satan says: "Doth Job fear God for nought?"

What Satan is doing here is basically accusing Job of being an opportunist. He asserts that Job only serves God because God does so much for him and blesses him so much. "Doth Job fear God for nought," means in our present day language something like this: "Job isn't serving you God for no reason." For nought, or nothing is how Satan put it. In other words, Job isn't serving you for nothing, God.

Doesn't that sound just like the enemy himself? Turning the tables to indicate that Job only serves God because God blesses Him? However, this idea is shattered by Job himself when he says in: **Job 1:21,** "And said, 'Naked came I out of my mother's womb, and naked shall I return thither: the Lord gave, and the Lord hath taken away; blessed be the name of the Lord.' "

When God said there were none like Him, He knew what He was talking about. I guess that this was the best Satan could do at the time. It is illustrations like this that demonstrate the nature of

Jerry McRaven

Satan in a way that he becomes even more loathsome to us than we thought he ever could.

Chapter Four

Introduction to the Hedge

Now we will move on to verse 10: Satan is asking the question: "Does Job fear God for nought?" Or, in other words, for (nothing)? Job:1:10, "Hast not thou made an hedge about him, and about his house, and about all that he hath on every side? Thou hast blessed the work of his hands, and his substance is increased in the land.' "

Now we are getting somewhere! Satan has just shown us his hand whether he intended to or not. We now know that he is frustrated with Job, and his true colors are beginning to emerge. God of course knew this, but Satan has unintentionally shown us why he hates Job. Satan hates to see God's people blessed.

We know that when God created Satan. He infused him with attributes like no other angel mentioned in Scripture. Satan is probably a "one of a kind" angel himself. But when it comes to attacking Job, he seems to be a bit desperate. No wonder he is frustrated, just listen to his description of Job:

He accuses God of making a hedge around Job.
This hedge extends around Job's house.
It extends around all that Job has.
It also extends around all the sides.
God blesses the works of his hands.
And God increases his substance in the land.

Can't you just hear Satan say: "It's no wonder Job serves you God, just look what you are doing for him!"

It surely appears to me that Satan is truly frustrated when it comes to attacking Job. Because God has placed a hedge of protection around him, around his house, around all that Job owns, all sides north, south, east, and west are all covered, God is continually blessing Job, and Job's substance is constantly being increased by God.

Satan seems convinced that God is somehow "overprotecting" Job from his attacks and to Satan this is totally unfair. Satan also asserts that Job's protection from him is "disproportionate" when compared with what Satan is allowed to do to others.

This is the first time Satan mentions that God has placed a "hedge" about Job. This hedge seems to protect Job from Satan's attacks somehow. As far as Satan is concerned, he is totally unable to penetrate through this God given hedge that is protecting Job from any and all attacks. Apparently, Satan has not encountered such a situation as this with anyone else. Only Job. Satan would admit himself, that Job truly is "unique" among men. He certainly has not found this to be the case with anyone else. There was no precedent for a hedge surrounding any known person or family on all sides that prohibited Satan from touching them, their substance or families. Now though, Satan had finally registered his major complaint against Job and made it known. Satan was unable to penetrate Job's hedge.

John 10:10, "The thief cometh not, but for to steal, and to kill, and to destroy: This is Satan's mission. He was complaining. He could not fulfill his mission against Job. His reasoning was because God was overprotecting Job with this hedge. I know I have heard ministers all my life teach on how God lifted Job's "hedge of protection." I do not believe that God lifted that hedge, and I don't find it in the Book of Job that God did. Later on, I will explain this in more detail.

Satan's mission is outlined in John 10:10. He comes to steal, to kill, and to destroy. This is what Satan does, and it is what he does best. His complaint to God was that he had absolutely no "access" to Job to fulfill his mission against him to steal, kill, and to destroy. According to Satan, this mission was impossible due to the hedge God had provided and afforded Job.

The very same scenario works for us. If Satan has no access to us, he can't harm us either. Satan cannot steal, kill, or destroy if there is no access to us. Satan must first have "access." Without access to us, Satan is helpless to inflict any damage or harm.

Job was protected on all sides with no access points anywhere. Satan made it very plain that he had absolutely no "points of entry" through the hedge God had provided. If you think about it, the construction of this hedge was quite a feat if Satan could not penetrate it anywhere or in anyway.

Please remember this truth: "The hedge itself was something that Satan was defeated by." Obviously Job or his family could not see it, as it was invisible to them. I seriously doubt that any of Job's neighbors or servants could see what made up this hedge.

Such facts seem to indicate to me that this hedge had a "spiritual" connotation to it, which explains why no one could see it, except for Satan. Satan most definitely knew of its existence, as he had encountered it whenever he came against Job. Satan did not however, explain to God the materials or elements God used to construct such a hedge. The fact that Job was perfect in his approach to serving God surely must have had something to do with it.

Satan was beside himself. Never before had he ever encountered such a hindrance or been blocked out by a hedge that somehow he could not penetrate or break through. Satan indicated that if the hedge was no longer in place protecting Job, that he could be successful against him. Satan understood that Job was indeed unique since he had no access to him and could not touch him. Only Job had such a hedge of protection.

Now we have reached the point that we must take a look and examine Satan's system.

-Satan's System-

We must understand that Satan operates within a specific framework or system. Understanding this, if we are to be successful against him, we must be totally aware of how he operates and we must know how to fight him. One would think that Job may have figured this out. Or, perhaps it was simply a by-product of Job being perfect in his approach to serving God! We shall see.

The first example of how Satan's system operates is found in Genesis chapter 3, in his account with Eve. This is the obvious place to start since it records a successful place where Satan employed his system to perfection. Satan "tempted" Eve and appealed to her flesh to "be as God," having her eyes opened.

When I see this account, I am drawn to two important aspects or points. The first is that Satan appealed to Eve's flesh through the vehicle of "temptation." He told Eve that she could be as God knowing good and evil. This reminds me that we have many TV preachers today teaching that we "are" Gods. They also say that Adam was not subservient to God, but was in all points his equal. My question to them would be: "If this is true, how could it possibly be a temptation to Adam or Eve to "be as God," if they were already like Him in all respects and in no way subordinate to Him being His equal? There would have been absolutely no temptation to be like Him since they were already like Him.

Nevertheless, Satan tempted Eve that she could be as God. The second point to be made is that Satan was restricted with Eve in temptation only. All Satan could do in this situation was tempt. He was not allowed to go any further than temptation itself. I submit that if Satan had been allowed to use a more powerful form of persuasion against Adam and Eve, he would have used it. But even in Satan's system, he is still subject to God's overall guidelines of which Satan can make no encroachment.

Satan must remain within the system God has set up. Satan is well aware of this and he wants to continue as a force against God, so he complies and remains within the ancient established prevailing standards. Because of this, Satan has become the "premiere" antagonist against us through his unmatched ability and his volumes of numerous temptation techniques and outright deceitfulness. Satan can go no further than tempting you to sin. Satan tried tempting Jesus in Matthew 4:1, "Then was Jesus led up of the Spirit into the wilderness to be tempted of the devil."

Jesus was tempted to turn stones into bread, and even during the crucifixion itself he was tempted to come down from the cross! The irony of it all, is that Jesus could have come down from the cross had He elected to do so. Remember what Jesus said when He was being arrested in the garden in **Matthew 26:53**, "Thinkest thou that I cannot now pray to my Father, and He shall presently give me more than twelve legions of angels?"

I am reminded in 2nd Kings, chapter nineteen, when one angel from the Lord killed 185,000 Assyrians. Twelve legions of angels amounts to 72,000 at a rate of 6,000 per legion. I did the math, this one angel slew the Assyrians at a rate of killing almost 4 Assyrians per second. At this rate, the entire Earth at that time would have been depopulated in less than twenty-four hours.

Jesus could have come down from the cross as it was within His power to do so, but the only thing that kept Him on the cross was His love for you and me. We were unable to redeem ourselves back to a righteous God. It took the sinless Son of God to be our substitute and take our sins as the Passover Lamb. Jesus redeemed us back to God by His shed blood.

Hebrews 4:15, "For we have not an high priest which cannot be touched with the feeling of our infirmities; but was in all points tempted like as we are, yet without sin." That pretty much says it all, doesn't it?

However, I submit to you, that if Christ had yielded to temptation, He would have sinned. If Jesus had yielded to temptation as we do, He would have acquired a sin nature like unto ours. Since Christ was a sinless sacrifice, He was acceptable to God as a sacrifice. Nobody else would have been able to atone for sin, except Jesus Christ. He was the only possible candidate to please God's requirement to take away our sins.

This is why Christ could say in John 14:30, "Hereafter I will not talk much with you: for the prince of this world cometh, and hath nothing in me." Jesus was plainly stating that Satan had no access to Him due to the fact He was without sin and had not taken on the nature of sin or Satan, like the rest of us have.

A small aside to this would be in **James 1:13**, "Let no man say when he is tempted, I am tempted of God: God cannot be tempted with evil, neither tempteth he any man." God may test you, as He did Abraham, but God will not tempt you. And God will not allow you to be tempted above that which you are able to stand.

We are never tempted by God. If and when we are tempted, we must remember that temptation is included in Satan's system. This is his way to try and persuade us to yield to his attempts, allowing him to gain access to us.

It is sometimes hard to understand, but it cannot be overlooked that Jesus' death was not like any other. Jesus did not die in the normal sense of the word. Yes, Jesus died alright, but there was nothing about His death which we could term as to be within the normal limits of what we know as the death experience.

First of all, the beating Jesus withstood by the wielding of the flagrum (sometimes called the cat of nine tails) and finally the crucifixion itself were necessary for Jesus to qualify for death. **Romans 6:23,** "For the wages of sin *is* death; but the gift of God *is* eternal life through Jesus Christ our Lord." All that you can earn from a life of sin is death. However, when we are referencing Jesus Christ, it must be noted that He has lived a life totally void of any sin and has remained pure to God and completely obedient to God's Word and instruction. Under such circumstances, He does not qualify for death.

It is only as Jesus becomes the substitute for the sins of the world that sin can be associated with Him at all. Christ personally was not a sinner, and He did not become a sinner while on the cross as some teach these days. Christ did not die spiritually, nor did He take on the nature of Satan or become "one" with Satan any more than the Passover lamb did.

If you are going to be executed for murder, and a person named William steps in and takes your place allowing you to go free, he becomes your substitute. He meets the requirement and obligation for payment of the crime. I reiterate that you are the guilty one, not William! William is not guilty, nor is he good for the crime. He simply takes your place and suffers your punishment for your crime. William does not become a murderer, simply because he is paying the required penalty for such a crime, and he does not become a criminal himself with evil desires.

Jesus did not become "one" with Satan on the cross, He merely stepped in and provided a way for us to live without a sin penalty. I understand our punishment for sin is not to die on a cross. However, this was where the blood was shed for sin, it wasn't in hell as some are saying these days. Jesus' body was not in hell; His Spirit was. The actual body of Christ remained in the tomb for the three days while He was in hell. How could Jesus shed blood in hell? He couldn't, nor could His Spirit shed any blood in hell, as it is the blood that removes sin. The cross was the location for payment of the sins of mankind.

Jesus is our Savior. Christ didn't suffer in hell for us, He suffered on the cross for us. When Christ went into hell, He was still God. Jesus never ceased to be God. In hell, He went straight to the gates and took the keys of death and of hell! Jesus was not born again as some teach. It was totally unnecessary for Christ to need a redeemer. He was sinless. Jesus paid the penalty for sin on the cross, not in hell. There are no scriptures that suggest Jesus suffered at all once He was removed from the cross. Jesus had a job to do and He did it. He took our sins, but was not guilty of any. It is like Jesus told the thief on the cross in **Luke 23:43**, "And Jesus said unto him, 'Verily I say unto thee, to day shalt thou be with me in paradise.' "

We must remember that our spirits are immortal. We will all live forever. Some of us will live with Christ in glorified bodies, and some of us will split hell wide open. No one is absent from being in hell as they are summoned to the Great White Throne Judgment, as hell is totally emptied out. **Romans 14:11**, "For it is written, '*As* I live, saith the Lord, every knee shall bow to me, and every tongue shall confess to God.' " We also have **Philippians 2:10**, "That at the name of Jesus every knee should bow, of *things* in heaven, and *things* in earth, and *things* under the earth;. . ."

Apparently all who have ever lived will bow their knees to Jesus Christ. I choose to bow to Jesus now, but others will do it later before being cast into hell. When Jesus died, it was only His earthly body, His Spirit didn't die, and we must remember that the Spirit of Jesus Christ is a "God" Spirit. Satan is not a God, nor are any of his fallen angels. Before Jesus was ever a man, He was God. Even while Jesus was in his human form, His Spirit remained the same. Remember the words of the evil spirits that spoke from inside a man in **Acts 19:15,** "And the evil spirit answered and said, 'Jesus I know, and Paul I know; but who are ye?'" Other demons said this to Jesus in **Mark 1:24,** "Saying, let *us* alone; what have we to do with thee, thou Jesus of Nazareth? Art thou come to destroy us? I know thee who thou art, the Holy One of God."

Jesus didn't need His physical body to defeat Satan in hell, He was a Spirit being long before He was in a human body. Jesus' Spirit never died. No spirit ever has. Even Goliath is alive somewhere today, but he has no physical body, and he never will have one again. This is what a demon is; it is a "disembodied spirit."

When Jesus said, "My God, my God, why has thou forsaken me?" He exited His body at that time because sin had separated Him from the Father which had never happened before. But it was not "his" sin. Once Jesus exited His body, His Spirit was back into communion with God immediately, as it was the literal, physical body of Christ, which had taken on the sins of the world. Jesus' Spirit was not touched by it. The spirit or conscious awareness if you will, of the Passover lamb had nothing to do with becoming sin, it was His body and blood that was needed for the symbolism.

We can't forget that Jesus was casting out devils as a human being. There is no record of anyone ever doing this before. Why did He have such authority? How was Christ more powerful than the demons while in human form? How come the demons knew who He was, and why did they fear Him? Simply because Jesus no longer remained in His human body is no reason His Spirit had deteriorated to the point He had lost His power over Satan. **Hebrews 13:8,** "Jesus Christ the same yesterday, and to day, and for ever."

John 10:17-18, "Therefore doth my Father love me, because I lay down my life, that I might take it again. **18** No man taketh it from me, but I lay it down of myself. I have power to lay it down, and I have power to take it again. This commandment have I received of my Father."

John 4:24, "God *is* a Spirit: and they that worship Him must worship *Him* in spirit and in truth."

In the original Greek, the article "a" is not present in John 4:24 which makes the reading to be: "God is Spirit," not 'a' spirit.

When Jesus became a man He was not manufactured as a new spirit, He was literally God in the flesh. **Matthew 1:23,** "Behold, a virgin shall be with child, and shall bring forth a son, and they shall call his name Emmanuel, which being interpreted is, God with us."

Jesus had the same Spirit He has always had. He did not receive a new one to be incarnated. He had authority over His body that we do not have. Explain the transfiguration if He didn't. Satan could not harm the Spirit of God in His body or out of it.

Jesus did not fear death, He knew exactly what would happen when He exited His earthly body, and He knew exactly what He would do and He did it. What Jesus did was something that only Jesus could do.

I know there is teaching out there these days indicating that any of the Old Testament prophets could have accomplished what Jesus did if only they had known what Jesus knew. This is error and hogwash, pure and simple.

Jerry McRaven

Chapter Five

The Proto-Evangelium

This is where the "proto-evangelium" comes into focus. This is merely a way to say: "the first gospel." It is found in: **Genesis 3:15,** "And I will put enmity between thee and the woman, and between thy seed and her seed; it shall bruise thy head, and thou shalt bruise his heel."

The verse introduces two elements previously unknown in the Garden of Eden. Elements which are the basis of Christianity — the curse on mankind because of Adam's sin and God's provision for a Savior from sin who would take the curse upon Himself.

This is truly the first gospel as it outlines for us the seed of the woman. Jesus is the only One who was qualified to redeem mankind. Jesus was absent of the sin nature, as He was not a sinner. Jesus is the only "seed of the woman." Reproductive science teaches the seed comes from the man, not the woman.

We also are aware that the fetus or infant child in the mother's womb does not come into direct contact with the blood of the mother. It is also a fact that the blood of the child comes from its father. **Matthew 1:18,** "Now the birth of Jesus Christ was on this wise: when as his mother Mary was espoused to Joseph, before they came together, she was found with child of the Holy Ghost." This begs the question: "Is the Holy Ghost God?" Yes, He is!

The Holy Spirit is a member of the triune Godhead, and the blood Jesus had in His body came from the Holy Spirit, not Mary, Joseph, or any other human being. This is why Jesus Christ is the only begotten Son of God. We as Christians are all sons of God, but we are not physically begotten of Him as Jesus was. Jesus is the only begotten Son of God; there are no others. Jesus is the only person to ever be "immaculately conceived." The blood of Jesus was pure. It had no impediments of sin, the curse, damaged DNA, generational discrepancies, disease, anemia, or any other abnormalities. It was pure and unadulterated. It was from God, how could it be unacceptable? For this reason, Jesus Christ of Nazareth, the Son of the living God, was the only sacrifice for sin that God the Father would accept.

Jesus "gave" His life; He did not just "die." **Mark 15:37,** "And Jesus cried with a loud voice, and gave up the ghost."

We also have in **Luke 23:46,** "And when Jesus had cried with a loud voice, He said, 'Father, into thy hands I commend my spirit,' and having said thus, He gave up the ghost." Jesus gave His spirit directly into the hands of God the Father. Jesus had the ability to exit His body with His spirit. Am I supposed to believe that God the Father turned Jesus over to be tortured in hell? I don't think so. We must notice that Jesus was in control. Jesus said: "Father into thy hands I commend my spirit." If we look closely at the entire crucifixion drama, Jesus was in total control throughout the entire ordeal. Besides, after Jesus gave His Spirit over to God, He gave up the ghost Himself.

Matthew 27:50, "Jesus, when He had cried again with a loud voice, yielded up the ghost." This occurred at the ninth hour. It was at this precise moment that the Passover lamb was being killed at the temple. It was also at this precise moment that the veil in the temple was torn. Since there was no sin in His life, Satan had no control over His death. Jesus died right on cue. At the precise moment the Passover lamb was being killed, Christ died.

I can't help but remember **Psalms 22:16,** "For dogs have compassed me: the assembly of the wicked have enclosed me: they pierced my hands and my feet." This scripture itself prophesied that Jesus would have His hands and feet pierced due to crucifixion. Since Satan is quite resourceful and discerning, he must have known the ramifications of this scripture and its meaning. However, he was totally powerless to stop it from happening even though he had over 1000 years to prepare to stop Jesus from going to the cross. Yes, it was Jesus that was in charge of the crucifixion, every step of the way.

It is my belief that Satan tried to stop Jesus from making it to the cross in the Garden of Gethsemane. I believe Satan tried to kill Jesus in the garden. Jesus said himself in **Matthew 26:38,** "Then saith He unto them, 'My soul is exceeding sorrowful, even unto death, tarry ye here, and watch with me.' " When Jesus says: "Even unto death," He is saying that He actually believes that He could possibly die from this. That is what even unto death means.

Luke the beloved physician said it like this: **Luke 22:44,** "And being in an agony He prayed more earnestly: and his sweat was as it were great drops of blood falling down to the ground." This is a condition known as diapedesis. It results from agitation of the nervous system, turning the blood out of its natural course, and forcing the red particles into the skin excretories. Similar cases throughout history have been recorded. (Note this: most notably when someone has been unjustly condemned to death.)

But in the case of Jesus, He was carrying the burden of the entire world upon His shoulders. No one had ever experienced such a thing before, or encountered such a burden. Mark says in **Mark 14:33,** "And He taketh with Him Peter and James and John, and began to be sore amazed, and to be very heavy;"

Try to explain to me what it means to be: "Sore Amazed!" I believe Mark was attempting to explain a situation that was life threatening and so physically challenging that He simply couldn't describe it with his vocabulary. I believe that when Jesus prayed for God to remove, "This Cup," He was not referencing the cross, but this situation He was experiencing in the garden itself.

Jesus had previously prophesied that He would be crucified, **Matthew 20:18-19,** "Behold, we go up to Jerusalem; and the Son of man shall be betrayed unto the chief priests and unto the scribes, and they shall condemn Him to death, **19** And shall deliver Him to the Gentiles to mock, and to scourge, and to crucify *Him*: and the third day He shall rise again."

Understanding this, how can Jesus now pray to escape the cross? If Jesus doesn't go to the cross, He has become a false prophet! What about John the Baptist that said, "Behold the lamb of God that taketh away the sin of the world?"

No my friend, Jesus must go to the cross. It is Satan that is trying to stop Jesus from making it to the cross by causing Him not to make it to Calvary. However, Jesus had prayed to God: Luke 22:41-43, "And He was withdrawn from them about a stone's cast, and kneeled down, and prayed, 42 Saying, Father, if thou be willing, remove (This Cup) from me: nevertheless not my will, but thine, be done." Jesus was not praying to escape the cross, He was praying for God to remove "this cup," of the heaviness, and from being "sore amazed" in the garden experience.

God did answer His prayer, by the way. Luke 22:43, "And there appeared an angel unto Him from heaven, (strengthening Him)." This was a direct answer to the prayer of Jesus. I don't know what this angel did to strengthen Jesus, but I know that He did somehow. The cup Jesus was drinking in the garden had become too much for Him to physically bear, and He needed strength. Thus the angel was dispatched from God to give Him strength and to keep Christ from harm. This was what Jesus asked for. He was strengthened as the angel was the answer to His prayer and gave Him strength to endure.

Jesus knew this angel. He had created Him. He knew the strength and power that He had placed within this angel, and all that this angel possessed. He knew He would come to no harm and that He was protected while He was in the arms of this powerful being. Jesus was not praying to escape the cross, He was praying to His Father in heaven so that He could endure the agony of the garden experience and still make it to the cross.

Jesus predicted He would be crucified. This means He had to go to the cross. Jesus also predicted He would be raised again on the 3rd day. This means He had to be resurrected because He had said it! "That it might be fulfilled which was spoken by the prophet."

Because of Psalm 22, and many other scriptures, Satan had over 1000 years to keep Jesus from going to the cross, but he was not able to stop Jesus from fulfilling prophecy. It was Jesus' desire to go to the cross and take our sins upon Himself that we as sinners could be reconciled back to a righteous and Holy God. Jesus did this through His blood atonement. It is not possible that anyone, other than Jesus Christ, could have accomplished this. Thank you Jesus! Remember what Jesus told Simon Peter in the garden: **John 18:11,** "Then said Jesus unto Peter, 'Put up thy sword into the sheath: the cup which my Father hath given me, shall I not drink it?'

Now that we have that all said, we must remember this one truth concerning Satan's system; beyond temptation, Satan is powerless to control or exercise authority over you. He uses temptation as a means to gain access, but only when we entertain his temptations can he gain access to kill, steal, and to destroy. Satan's system is designed to gain access to you, and to gain entry through the hedge of protection, providing you have a hedge in the first place.

Now it is time to examine God's system. We know God has one, and we know certain details about it, so let's take a look. Surely, one would think God's system must be very detailed and complicated.

-God's System-

God's system is not complicated at all. On the contrary, God's system is very simple. There is only one major aspect or design as it relates to God's system. Here it is:

Sin Must Be Covered!

That's it! I told you it was simple. After all, what did Jesus come to do but to take away our sins?

The difference in Job's sacrifices and what Jesus did is that Job's sacrifice could only "cover" a person's sins, while Jesus and His death on the cross as the sinless Lamb of God actually "takes away" our sins forever.

Even today, in God's eyes, there are only two types of people on the Earth. Believe it or not, but that is a true statement. We have those whose sins have not been covered by blood, and those who have been covered.

When God looks at you or me, He either sees sin, or He sees your sins have been taken away by the blood of Jesus on the cross. There are no other options. We would call those people whose sins have been taken away, and not just covered: saved.

Often in church circles we speak about a person being saved or not saved. **Romans 10:9-10,** "That if thou shalt confess with thy mouth the Lord Jesus, and shalt believe in thine heart that God hath raised Him from the dead, thou shalt be saved. **10** For with the heart man believeth unto righteousness; and with the mouth confession is made unto salvation."

Paul is explaining to us here how we can be saved by belief in Jesus Christ and His being raised from the dead. John explains what it is that saves us and takes away our sins: **1 John 1:7,** "But if we walk in the light, as He is in the light, we have fellowship one with another, and the blood of Jesus Christ his Son cleanseth us from all sin." It is the blood of Jesus that cleanses us from sin. It is not anything we can do for ourselves that can do this; it takes the blood of Jesus.

God's system dictates that sin must be covered somehow. We know that Jesus can take away our sins by His blood, but let's look at what was done prior to Christ and His sacrifice on the cross. I guess that a good place to start would be at the beginning, so let's do just that.

God's system actually begins in Genesis 3:21, "Unto Adam also and to his wife did the Lord God make coats of skins, and clothed them." Something died, and blood was shed. This single act is where "The Thread of Blood" woven throughout all of Scripture actually begins. The fig leaves that Adam and Eve had made were not good enough, blood had to be shed to cover their sin.

Genesis 4:3-4, "And in process of time it came to pass, that Cain brought of the fruit of the ground an offering unto the Lord. **4** And Abel, he also brought of the firstlings of his flock and of the fat thereof. And the Lord had respect unto Abel and to his offering."

Now, it is easy to see why Cain's offering was not accepted by God. It was a bloodless offering. Cain no doubt brought the very best of his produce, but God was not pleased. The flip side of this is that Abel brought of the firstlings of his flock. Abel didn't bring the old and worn out of his flock, but the firstlings. Abel's offering was of blood, and this is why God had respect to it. God told Cain that if he did well, he also would be accepted.

You can actually see results of God's system at work in: Leviticus 26:3-4, "If ye walk in my statutes, and keep my commandments, and do them; then I will give you rain in due season, and the land shall yield her increase, and the trees of the field shall yield their fruit."

Doesn't this remind you of what was happening with Job? Remember that Job was perfect and upright and that there were none like Him. Job was perfect in his approach to serving God. Job was truly walking in God's statutes and keeping God's commands. As a result of Job's compliance with God's statutes, God gave him rain in due season, the land yielded her increase, and the trees of the field yielded their fruit also. It was because of God's blessing of Job that Satan was initially complaining.

By the time you read down to Leviticus 26:9, God says this in **Leviticus 26:9,** "For I will have respect unto you, and make you fruitful, and multiply you, and establish my covenant with you."

Certainly Job had become fruitful and he was being multiplied by God on every side. It would be difficult for me to believe that God would punish Job and allow Satan to penetrate the hedge while Job is being obedient to God's statutes and compliant with all God's commandments. Job had earned God's respect, but did Job have a covenant with God as he mentions here? And if he did, what was it?

Now God has introduced something new. In Leviticus 26:9, He said He would establish "His covenant" with them. So the question is: "What is this all important covenant that God made with Abraham and his descendants?" Remembering that Abraham was Jacob's grandfather, the covenant God made with Abraham would be the same one as Job would be observing. We know this since Jacob was Job's grandfather. So, what was this covenant?

Genesis 17:10, "This is my covenant, which ye shall keep, between me and you and thy seed after thee; every man child among you shall be circumcised." God's covenant with Abraham and his descendants was the covenant of circumcision. Without going into great detail, we know that circumcision is a covenant of blood. We also know that Job would have kept this covenant since He was perfect and upright, fearing God and eschewing evil. Since Job was perfect in his approach to serve God, he certainly would have kept the covenant of circumcision God had established with Abraham, Isaac, and Jacob.

God not only established His covenant of blood with Abraham, Isaac, and Jacob, He established this covenant with their descendants as well. We know that God established His covenant of circumcision with Abraham, and that this covenant is a covenant of blood. We also know that later when Moses was leading Israel out of Egyptian bondage, God established the "Passover."

The Passover did not change the covenant of circumcision, but it did establish the first of the seven feasts, that of Passover. It set into motion the blood of protection for Israel. God said: "When I see the blood I will pass over you." We know the blood was sprinkled over the door posts from the Passover lamb. This blood protected the Israelites from the destroyer, which came through and killed all the firstborn in every home in the land of Egypt that didn't have the blood sprinkled upon the door posts. It also established the first of God's seven feast days. Jesus would be crucified on this day about 1,500 years later. Jesus would become our Passover lamb as He would provide for us a blood covering as did the Passover lamb for the Israelites while leaving Egyptian bondage.

Jerry McRaven

Chapter Six

The Power of the Blood

Exodus 12:7, "And they shall take of the blood, and strike it on the two side posts and on the upper door post of the houses, wherein they shall eat it." Blood is an inescapable part of God's system! As we can see, God had established a covenant of blood with the children of Israel through circumcision. God also established it again, later, in the keeping of the Passover sacrifice and the covering of safety.

When you look at the symbolism of the Passover itself, with the sprinkling of the blood on the door posts, the three points for the blood were atop the door post and on either side, making the three points of the cross. This symbolism continues with the fact that it was only the blood of the Passover lamb that could be used. And finally, this blood had the power to protect those under its application.

The power of the blood from the Passover lamb had the ability to "save" you from the destroyer that sought to kill you. This is very powerful in its reality and symbolism. It is also remarkable that the Passover lamb by necessity was required to be: without spot, or blemish. It had to be a "perfect" sacrifice!

The entire Book of Leviticus is centered around the laws concerning sacrifices and offerings. Virtually all of these sacrifices mentioned were blood sacrifices as were almost all of the offerings. These offerings were a type or shadow of Jesus Christ and His perfect and ultimate sacrifice. All of the Old Testament offerings and sacrifices were symbolic of the personal offering Jesus Christ would make for the world. This symbolism cannot be overlooked. We sometimes forget the power of symbolism in scripture. Symbolism is a very powerful tool that God uses. For instance, think of Abraham offering his only son as a sacrifice to illustrate God offering his only son as a sacrifice for the world. When you think about it, many of us would give ourselves as a sacrifice for someone, but we would not give the life of our only son. You may be willing to sacrifice yourself, but we don't offer up our only son. We also see the symbolism of Jesus the "Passover lamb," and Barabbas, the "scapegoat." Jesus was crucified, and Barabbas was set free.

God was then and is now a God of covenant. Whether you like it or not, God's covenant is a covenant of blood. This is a subject seldom mentioned in many of our churches these days.

Crosses are being removed in order to become more "seeker friendly." Preachers are not elaborating on the blood of Jesus, but are instead giving us great motivational sermons on helping others and doing good things for our communities. Sin is not something preached against or even mentioned as it has "negative connotations" and can be construed as not bolstering our "self-esteem," and it is also considered to be judgmental.

We don't want anyone in our congregation to be offended. We want people to feel comfortable in our church, so we will not preach anything that might bring into question certain standards of living that could possibly be construed as being a reproof or rebuke. We are not going to discuss behaviors or personal weaknesses, as that might not stimulate church growth. This is why we now have a large "social gospel" contingency.

Many of our new churches are concentrating on the "treasure" that is within all of us, while the Bible says our heart is desperately wicked who can know it? Since we have a sin nature, what do we have that God would want or desire to use?

It just so happens that God is still a God of covenant, and His covenant is one of blood. You cannot remove the blood from this covenant and expect it to have any power.

This explains why many of today's churches have a form of godliness, but deny the power of God. We have "green" churches, lesbian churches, gay churches, White churches, Black churches, Hispanic churches, Oriental churches, Drive-through churches, internet churches, and even Cowboy churches. I am thinking of starting a baseball church, or a trout fisher's church. My wife Janice could possibly start a "seamstress" church. Isn't this ridiculous? Why do we continue to divide the body of Christ?

Aren't there enough divisive elements in the church world already? However, if someone finds Christ through such means, so be it.

It makes no difference what kind of church you choose to attend, the fact remains and always will, that if you are to receive salvation it will be through the shed blood of Jesus Christ and not some religious motivational gymnastics or anything else that comes down the proverbial pike.

Jesus said in **John 10:9,** "I am the door: by me if any man enter in, he shall be saved, and shall go in and out, and find pasture." Jesus also said in **John 14:6,** "Jesus saith unto him, 'I am the way, the truth, and the life: no man cometh unto the Father, but by me.'"

I admit I may not be the sharpest knife in the drawer, and coming from the "sticks" in Missouri, we are sometimes typecast as simple or unlearned. But I am aware of the fact that Jesus is not a "physical" door even though He said He was one. I understand the symbolism or figurative speech used here. However, I do know that if you are to reach heaven you will have to go through the shed blood of Jesus to get there. Such an act in itself actually makes Jesus Christ the doorway to salvation.

Acts 4:12, "Neither is there salvation in any other: for there is none other name under heaven given among men, whereby we must be saved." I think that is quite plain enough for even a "hick" from the Ozarks of Missouri to understand.

All I am trying to disclose is that when you take the blood out of the church, you will also strip that church of any real power.

The Gospel According to Job

You just can't remove the blood from God's covenant and expect it to have any power since there is "Power in the blood!" As a result, some of today's churches actually symbolize Cain more than Abel.

This explains why a large dose of today's new gospel and many of our radio and (TV) preachers have no power in their churches! It is like trying to start your car without a battery. No power. You might be able to push your car to start it, or you could have someone to "jump start" it. Either way, you can still drive, but you don't have any power when you need it.

Many of today's churches must depend on an outside source or authority for their power. It might be a denomination, or a TV preacher, an author or a book, a certain leader, a big bank account, a specific church or church pastor, a church membership, or it could even be a tradition or custom. Possibly it could depend upon their "good works." Catholics may depend on reciting "Hail Mary's," Rosaries, or even Mother Mary herself, of which scripture makes no mention as it pertains to spiritual power.

God will not and cannot violate the terms of His covenant. Absolutely everything you will ever need is provided for you within the terms of God's covenant that Christ made for us on the cross. God's covenant is a blood covenant and if you plan to please God, you will accept His terms. You will not be successful by opting out of God's covenant for something else that He has not approved or mandated.

God will not accept Mohammed, Buddha, Confucius, Zoroaster, the Dalai Lama, your astrological chart, Hari Krishna, or anyone else. It is Jesus Christ and Him crucified. Period. The last time I noticed, Jesus is the only one of all the rest that died for our sins and said He would raise Himself from the dead and did it. Jesus is now sitting at the right hand of the throne of God interceding for us to the Father while the Holy Spirit dwells and works within His church here on the Earth.

It is paramount to this message that we understand the blood that Job had access to through his many sacrifices and offerings was "symbolic." There truly was nothing special about the blood that Job sacrificed. All of Job's offerings simply "pointed to" the coming perfect sacrifice of the Son of God. **Hebrews 10:4,** "For *it is* not possible that the blood of bulls and of goats should take away sins."

This was pure symbolism. Just like the Passover lamb symbolized Christ, the many sacrifices Job made were symbolic of what Jesus would do once and for all with the sacrifice of himself. Even so, don't forget that the blood of the Passover lamb was powerful enough to save all persons within the house to which it was applied.

Today, we don't have symbolic blood, nor do we need to make any more sacrifices. When Jesus said: "It is finished," He wasn't just making a reference to His death on the cross, but to the entire system of the redemption of mankind. Jesus had paid the full price God required to bring a sinful man back to himself through this act of reconciliation. The writer of Hebrews says it best in **Hebrews 10:10,** "By the which will we are sanctified through the offering of the body of Jesus Christ once *for all*." Notice here, that it is the offering of the physical "body" of Christ, not His spirit.

Regarding Heb. 10:10, I do believe once means once and all means all. This is why I don't believe I need to do anything else. My salvation has been purchased for me. All of my "works" will fall quite short of Jesus' finished work on the cross. I do need to repent of my sins, and ask the Lord Jesus to take my sins away by His cleansing blood.

I need to confess Jesus as my Lord and Savior, and give my life to Him for His service. Today, it seems everyone regardless of what type of church they attend want Jesus to be their Savior. But that seems to be as far as it goes. People realize they need a Savior, but for some reason they don't think they need, nor do they want Him as "Lord." Jesus is not only my Savior; He is my Lord and Savior. I wouldn't have or want it any other way.

It sometimes is frustrating to see the proverbial "bumper sticker" which quips: "Jesus is my co-pilot." Well, Jesus is my pilot. I am along for the ride and I am going where He is going, wherever that may be. Christ is in charge and we need to conform to His will.

Do you remember how Satan was accusing Job and saying that he was so blessed and God had placed a hedge of protection around him? I submit to you that the hedge of protection around Job was formed in Job 1:5.

Job 1:5, "And it was so, when the days of *their* feasting were gone about, that Job sent and sanctified them, and rose up early in the morning, and offered burnt offerings *according* to the number of them all: for Job said, 'It may be that my sons have sinned, and cursed God in their hearts.' Thus did Job continually." We sometimes neglect to see important facts from scripture that may seem unimportant to us, but they can be very salient to the intended meaning. For instance, here in Job 1:5, it mentions that Job sanctified his sons and "rose up early in the morning."

To many reading this, it is only a statement of fact about the time of day. I personally think it is much more than that. Job was rising early to sacrifice his burnt offerings. This indicates to me that Job didn't want much time to elapse before he could prepare an appropriate sacrifice after the fact.

Job was not in the habit of being hindered by anything when it came to making his sacrifices in a very timely manner. Again, as far as Job was concerned, if a sin had been committed, or even if a sin was "rumored," Job wasted no time in preparing the proper sacrifice for it. It was a constant cycle. If there was a sin, there was a sacrifice quickly thereafter to cover it. We cannot allow ourselves to ever forget that all of Job's sacrifices and offerings were blood offerings and sacrifices.

Job would offer his sacrificial offerings for each of his children. It says in verse 5: "To the number of them all," which simply means that Job sacrificed an offering for each of his children and left none of them out of the process. Job said: "It may be that my sons have sinned, and cursed God in their hearts."

The Gospel According to Job

This is very important to note: Job was sure to make a sacrifice "just in case" one of his sons had sinned or cursed God without his knowledge. Job was taking no chances. Blood was going to be shed for each of Job's children in a very timely manner. This fact was not up for debate.

However, in my humble opinion, one of the most important aspects of Job 1:5 is where the verse makes the declaration about the sins, followed immediately by the sacrifices, and that this cycle constantly keeps forever reproducing itself. He did this continually. He never stopped the shedding of blood over his family. Job must have somehow understood the concept about the blood sacrifice.

Usually a hedge or a fence is placed up to protect someone or something. A hedge or fence can also simply be a border for your property. If the fence or hedge is a border, it is also there for a reason - to keep people out. However, when you come to a hedge, if you are to penetrate through it, you must somehow negotiate your way inside.

You have several options open to you. You can try to go over it, under it, push it over, possibly go around it, and maybe through it. How you gain entry is totally up to you, as it is also dependent upon the nature or design of the hedge itself. The hedge may be too high to go over. It also may be too strong to push over or too embedded in the ground to go under it. It could be too thick to go through, or too far to go around.

Since we don't know the material that constructed the hedge Job had, it is difficult to try to figure a way inside of it. However, it should be discussed that when one encounters a hedge, you do not just sit down and make yourself comfortable and wait for someone from the inside to come and let you in. The hedge is there for a reason, and that reason is to keep people like you out!

This reminds me of the idea that a fox is trying to penetrate a hedge-like barrier to gain access to the chicken house inside. The fox does not just lie down and take a nap waiting for you to come and let him inside, now does he? He tries for all he is worth to breach the integrity of the hedge somehow to gain access to one of the succulent fowls in the chicken house. Mr. Farmer, or owner of the chicken house is not going to give access to the fox or any other predator for any reason and under any circumstances.

Why would we then think that God would just give Satan access to Job simply because he was frustrated by the hedge? In considering this, especially when we realize that Job was perfect in his approach to serve God? Job was being blessed because he was compliant with God's statutes. God did not remove Job's hedge of protection. If we would just remember, the hedge had to be a spiritual one, since there was no obvious "natural materials" or visible construction. Other than God and the angels, Satan and his henchmen were the only ones that knew of the hedge's existence. Even Job himself couldn't see it.

Satan is no different than any fox or other predator. Satan must have looked diligently to find a way inside the hedge, but he was

The Gospel According to Job

obviously unsuccessful and to no avail. We don't know how many times Satan tried to breach the hedge, nor do we know how long it had been since he had first encountered it. What we do know is this: Satan complained about the hedge and stated that he could not penetrate it. We know that Satan thought that Job was being overprotected and that God should give him access. Satan desperately wanted the hedge out of his way.

This is a picture of the way Satan operates. He wants access to you because you are a child of God. We are Christians, and Satan wants to kill, steal, and destroy us.

Isaiah 59:19 states, "So shall they fear the name of the Lord from the west, and his glory from the rising of the sun. When the enemy shall come in like a flood, the spirit of the Lord shall lift up a standard against him.

The "standard" referenced here is a flag. God will raise the flag against our enemies. Just what flag do you suppose that might be? I think it is the flag of the blood of our Lord and Savior Jesus Christ, the Son of the living God!

Remember how Job was constantly shedding blood? "Thus did Job continually." I am a firm believer that continually means continually. This means Job was constantly shedding blood for himself and his family. There was not a day that went by that Job didn't sacrifice or make a burnt offering. Thus did Job continually! This is the key!

I submit to you that Job's hedge was created in Job 1:5: "And it was so, when the days of *their* feasting were gone about, that Job sent and sanctified them, and rose up early in the morning, and offered burnt offerings *according* to the number of them all: for Job said, 'It may be that my sons have sinned, and cursed God in their hearts.' Thus did Job continually."

Chapter Seven

Creation of the Hedge

Since Job left out none of his children, or any family members as he included them all when he sacrificed, and since Job continually sacrificed every day and was in a constant state of sacrificing burnt offerings to God, the constant shedding of blood over Job and his family created this hedge of protection.

This is the very same concept of the Passover. "When I see the blood, I will pass over you." It is the blood. The blood is our protection. Why are we saved if it isn't by the blood shed by our Savior on Calvary's cross! Think about it. All of Job's sacrifices were purely symbolic of what Jesus would do on the cross. Basically, they were rehearsals.

Since the blood Job had was powerful, just think what the blood of Jesus Christ can do! Job was trusting symbolic blood. We have the actual blood of Jesus to protect us! It is certain that if Satan could not penetrate the hedge of symbolic blood, he will not try to pass the bloodline of the precious blood of Jesus. Thank you Jesus!

Job was continually covering himself and his family in blood! It was the blood that created the hedge. Just as it is the blood of Jesus that creates a hedge of protection around us today! This explains to me why God didn't "lift" the hedge around Job. How can anyone justify God lifting the protection afforded us by the blood of Christ? The price for our "hedge" of protection is too high for God to simply lift it and give Satan access. Besides, in Malachi 3:11 God says He will rebuke the devourer for your sake, when you give God what He requires. Job most certainly was giving God what He required.

Satan will also not even attempt to cross the bloodline. If he wouldn't try the blood of oxen, sheep, and goats, he certainly will not endeavor to proceed through the blood of Jesus Christ. The blood of Jesus is without a doubt the most powerful substance in the universe. It has the power to TAKE AWAY SINS. Satan won't touch it.

Leviticus 17:11, "For the life of the flesh *is* in the blood: and I have given it to you upon the altar to make an atonement for your souls: for it *is* the blood *that* maketh an atonement for the soul."

The blood of Jesus represents the very life essence of the Incarnate Christ. The life is in the blood. Satan cannot cross the bloodline of Jesus Christ, nor will He try. We have the power of the blood of Jesus working for us.

Repeating Leviticus 17:11, "For the life of the flesh *is* in the blood: and I have given it to you upon the altar to make an atonement for your souls: for it *is* the blood *that* maketh an atonement for the soul."

Yes, it is the "blood" that makes atonement for us, and the "life" is in the blood. Once the blood has been removed from the church, the "life" of the church is gone. The absence of life within the church means the church is dead and powerless. A dead body cannot "rise and walk" or function as intended.

1 Peter 1:18-20, "Forasmuch as ye know that ye were not redeemed with corruptible things, *as* silver and gold, from your vain conversation *received* by tradition from your fathers; **19** But with the precious blood of Christ, as of a lamb without blemish and without spot: **20** Who verily was foreordained before the foundation of the world, but was manifest in these last times for you, . . ."

The blood of Jesus was manifested for us. We can't be saved or receive salvation without it. If you are to be saved and go to Heaven upon your death, it will be the blood of Jesus that affords you entrance into the abode of God. Nothing else can gain you entrance. Your good works will not be able to get you in, nor can anything else. Your church, your denomination, your favorite TV preacher, your doctorate of divinity, super bowl ring, or your academy award will not do it either.

John 10:1, "Verily, verily, I say unto you, he that entereth not by the door into the sheepfold, but climbeth up some other way, the same is a thief and a robber."

In Bible times, there was only one way into the sheepfold. The sheep knew this way, and they felt safe. We know Jesus is the door, and He is explaining that He is the same as the sheepfold. There is only one way there, and anyone entering into the sheepfold any other way was a thief and a robber.

There are not "many" ways to God as some are teaching these days. I have heard it declared by well-respected scholars that there are 3 ways to God: Christianity, Judaism, and Islam. I must disagree.

Let us continue now with **Job 1:11:** "But put forth thine hand now, and touch all that he hath, and he will curse thee to thy face." One observation about this verse that I must make. God certainly knew Job better than Satan did, because what Satan said Job would do was not what Job did!

Satan has just now made God an offer that He can't refuse. The enemy of our souls is so confident that he thinks if he can gain access to us, he will be successful to kill, steal, and to destroy. But in this instance, Satan makes a bold statement about Job. Satan basically is making the prediction that if Job didn't have his possessions and if you take away all he has been blessed with, he will curse God to His face. Apparently, Satan feels strongly about this as he has "laid it on the line" so to speak.

I can only conjecture that the reason Satan is so confident about this proposal is because he had never failed with anyone before. Satan feels if the hedge is gone, and Job loses everything, he will react in the same manner as everyone else would. Satan seems to have forgotten what God said in: **Job 1:8,** "And the Lord said unto Satan, hast thou considered my servant Job, that *there is* none like Him in the earth, a perfect and an upright man, one that feareth God, and escheweth evil?"

That there is none like him in the Earth is quite a powerful statement. Again, he is perfect and upright. It appears that Satan is in for a big surprise. There can actually be someone in the Earth with honesty, integrity, character, and a changed heart who truly loves and obeys God.

Hebrews 11:6, "But without faith *it is* impossible to please *Him*: for he that cometh to God must believe that He is, and *that* He is a rewarder of them that diligently seek Him."

I believe that Job had faith. Again, I actually believe that Job may have understood the concept of the ritual of burnt offerings and the shedding of blood. We will discuss this later in this book.

We are now getting into the heart of this message, and things are beginning to move rather quickly. For this reason, I will attempt to make precise illustrations as to what is taking place in the dialogue or narrative. Things are now starting to get quite interesting.

As previously mentioned I had gone through the Book of Job many, many times, but never "saw" what I am relating to you before, nor have I heard others teach it. I pray that it does for you what it has for my wife and myself and others that have already heard it.

We are coming now to Job 1:12, which is a very "key" verse. This verse needs a little explaining, so stay with me.

Job 1:12, "And the Lord said unto Satan, Behold, all that he hath *is* in thy power; only upon himself put not forth thine hand. So Satan went forth from the presence of the Lord."

We must pay close attention to this verse. On the outset, it seems that God has "lifted" the hedge and given Satan unrestricted access to Job. However, that is not what is going on here, let me explain.

God says: "Behold, all that he hath is in thy power." God is not throwing Job under the bus here! Instead, He is giving Satan some very detailed and precise instructions. God has told Satan to "Behold" Job. Let's take a look.

When God gave me this "revelation" about Job, He impressed upon me in verse 12 to "obey the punctuation." I know this may sound strange, but I seem to remember somewhere, something about a jot and tittle, which were very small grammatical marks used in ancient writing. A jot in Greek is often linked to the word: "iota." **Matthew 5:18,** "For verily I say unto you, till heaven and earth pass, one jot or one tittle shall in no wise pass from the law, till all be fulfilled."

Now that God has instructed me to obey the punctuation, I look at the word "Behold" and observe it to be followed by a comma. I have always been told to use a comma before a "pause."

Therefore, in obeying the punctuation as God impressed me to do, I again looked at verse 12: **Job 1:12,** "And the Lord said unto Satan, Behold, all that he hath *is* in thy power; only upon himself put not forth thine hand. So Satan went forth from the presence of the Lord."

"And the Lord said unto Satan, (comma). So I paused. After the word: "Behold" appears another (comma), so I paused again. So, this is what it seemed to me like what God wanted me to discover:

"And the Lord said unto Satan, ...Behold, ... all that he hath is in thy power."

After pausing correctly, I realized something that I probably would not have discovered had I not obeyed the punctuation.

It is the word "Behold." So, I looked up the word Behold in Hebrew to find something amazing. The Hebrew word for behold is the word: "Hinneh." Its meaning helped me to understand what God was telling Satan to do. Behold in this sense means to "look." The Hebrew lexicon mentions that the insertion of this word often marks a change in viewpoint.

Heb. Hinneh: to look, to behold, lo (which means to look), indeed, here, look here, go, <u>go look</u>, see, if he sees, surely, now, there, unless, after all, etc.

Hinneh is used elsewhere in the Book of Job, so I "looked" to see how it was used: **Job 40:15-16,** "Behold now behemoth, which I made with thee; he eateth grass as an ox. **16** Lo now, his strength *is* in his loins, and his force *is* in the navel of his belly."

In verse 15, God is instructing Job to "look" at the behemoth. "See" that he eats grass as an ox. In verse 16 God says: "Lo" now or "look now" that his strength is in his loins, and his force is in the navel of his belly. Wasn't God instructing Job to look at the behomoth? He eats grass, doesn't he? Look!

By using the word "Behold" God was giving Satan an instruction to do something. He was being told to: "Go and look," of which both words are used in hinneh as definitions.

I continued to investigate this even further and came to the following conclusion. I strongly believe that what God was doing in verse 12 was to instruct Satan to go and look closely at Job. I even believe as I studied further that the instruction actually given to Satan was for him to actually do the following:

Satan was instructed to behold Job. (Heb. "Hinneh")

1. Hinneh means to behold (Job).
2. It means to look at closely, to study (Job).
3. To actually discern or see Job for what he was.
4. It means to consider or examine Job and what he does.
5. To pay respect to and to scrutinize (Job).
6. It means to actually perceive who Job was.
7. To regard and pay close attention to (Job).
8. It means to take heed to (Job) and his way of doing things.

9. To watch Job intently.
10. It even means to actually spy on (Job).
11. It also means to look well to (Job).
12. To closely observe (Job).

I think this sheds more light on when God asked Satan: "Have you CONSIDERED my servant Job that there is none like him in the earth." This statement implied by God suggests Satan's investigation of Job may not have been quite thorough enough.

John 19:5, "Then came Jesus forth, wearing the crown of thorns, and the purple robe. And Pilate saith unto them, 'Behold the man!' " Just what exactly was Pilate telling the crowd to do here? Of course the word "Behold" is a Greek word in the New Testament, but it means the same thing, "Behold, look, lo, see."

Obviously Pilate was instructing the crowd to "look intently" at Jesus. His point being that Jesus was already so physically damaged from the flagrum and whipping post, it was doubtful He could survive anyway, so why the necessity to crucify Him.

Besides, how would Satan know what God was asking him to do if he hadn't already investigated Job thoroughly? Satan knew exactly what God was saying. He knew that if he wanted access to Job, and if he wanted entry through the hedge of protection, he had to go and investigate Job again, more thoroughly to find it. After all, God had said, "Behold all that he hath is in your power."

Now, let's go back to: Job 1:12, "And the Lord said unto Satan, 'Behold, all that he hath is in thy power; only upon himself put not forth thine hand. So Satan went forth from the presence of the Lord." It was at this time that Satan left to <u>begin a complete and comprehensive case study of Job.</u>

Satan now knew that there was a way inside the hedge, and he was determined to find it. God didn't just turn Job over to be destroyed by Satan. God does not do this or allow the enemy such access when we are perfect in our approach to serving Him. God would also not be honoring His Word if He allowed Satan access. However, there is nothing unusual or untoward about God instructing Satan that if you want access to Job, you are going to have to go find it for yourself, as I am not going to give it to you or explain to you how to get it. Such is perfectly within the legal boundaries God had set up between Himself and Satan.

When we last left Satan, he was just embarking on his complete case study of Job. He was determined to find access because he had been denied all access to employ his tactics to kill, steal, and destroy.

I believe we can safely assume that Satan did not discover his access point of entry to Job in one day, two days, or a week. We don't know how long it took, but we can be reasonably sure that it could have covered a substantial period of time. In any event, we do know that Satan diligently began his investigation.

Now we can advance to **Job 1:13**: "And there was a day when his sons and his daughters *were* eating and drinking wine in their eldest brother's house:"

Just by the appearance and nature of this verse, we are led to believe that there had been some time elapse from the time Satan left from the presence of the Lord to begin his intense case study of Job.

"And there was a day," begins verse 13. I submit this was the day Satan made his discovery. I believe Satan saw the whole system at work on this particular day. And there was a day (when.) The word "when" here is significant. This day and this time now becomes our focus. Because on this day, Job's sons and daughters were eating and drinking wine in their eldest brothers house. From the narrative itself, we are told that Job's sons and daughters are engaged in the very act of drinking wine at their eldest brothers place of habitation. It is something they are involved with and doing at the very moment being described. They were actively engaged in these activities on this day "when" Satan figured out the system. Because of these events, and what he has observed, Satan now knows: "How The System Works!"

Right now would be a very opportune time to contrast verse 5 and verse 13 to help illustrate what is taking place. I know I have used this verse a number of times, but this should be the last: **Job 1:5,** "And it was so, when the days of *their* feasting were gone about, that Job sent and sanctified them, and rose up early in the morning, and offered burnt offerings *according* to the number of them all: for Job said, it may be that my sons have sinned, and cursed God in their hearts. Thus did Job continually."

It speaks of their days of feasting and that they are "gone about." The idea here is that there would likely be a birthday festival or other celebration. Job then sent for and sanctified them. Job always rose up early in the morning to prepare the burnt offerings to prevent any enemy from attempting to delay or impede the sacrifice process. Apparently Job was sending for his sons and daughters and calling out their names one by one to God as he would prepare the sacrifices for each of them. For this specific number of sacrifices Job would need the help and assistance of his many servants as this is quite an undertaking since Job had 7 sons and 3 daughters.

Job 1:13, "And there was a day when his sons and his daughters *were* eating and drinking wine in their eldest brother's house:"

The difference in verse 5 and here, is that these celebrations were in progress, and Job had not begun the process for sacrifice as yet. There is no record that these activities were being sacrificed for at this time, and it doesn't seem to be early in the morning, since the sons and daughters were presently in their eldest brothers home celebrating.

At this juncture I must make a clarification of 2 specific points that pertained to Job that are different today.

Chapter Eight

Two Important Points

Point #1

Job lived in a time where we must first imagine a world without any scripture whatsoever! There is no Bible. All the knowledge Job had concerning spiritual things had been handed down to him by his fathers. As far as we know, there were no written laws or instructions regarding sacrifices and offerings. A list of Job's patriarchal fathers would include: Adam, Abel, Noah, Shem, and more recently, Abraham, Isaac, and Jacob. There is no law of Moses, and there are no Ten Commandments. There is nothing specific that we know of for Job to use as a guide. The only guideline for Job is that he knows from the very beginning that only a blood offering or sacrifice is acceptable. There is no "Passover" as it hasn't happened yet. The only example Job has is to prepare an offering of blood. This is all he knows.

Point #2

We must understand that this is a totally different "dispensation." We know that God has dealt differently with people throughout history. Such time periods are known as dispensations. Job however, lived under the "dispensation of promise" and was obligated to sacrifice blood. Job also as the high priest of his household could make sacrifices for his entire family.

The actual laws that applied to Job are not the same that govern us today, and many no longer apply. For instance, Job was required to make sacrifices to cover his sins, and those of his household. Today, we are not required to make any blood offerings. This is because we now live under the "dispensation of grace" and sacrifices are now over.

The dispensation of promise was then followed by the "dispensation of law" established by Moses. The dispensation of law replaced the dispensation of promise, and superseded it, giving us the Ten Commandments. However, all Job knew was what he had either seen or been taught. Job knew that Abel sacrificed blood and was respected for it, and it was in this area that Job was perfect before God. -End of the two points-

Again, allow me to say that I believe Job understood his actions in the sacrifice forum. Job seemed to know that he was only doing rehearsals for a "perfect" sacrifice that would someday come. Job addresses this very concept when he said in:

The Gospel According to Job

Job 19:25, "For I know that my redeemer liveth, and that He shall stand at the latter day upon the earth:"

How did Job know this unless he had the revelation from God to know? I challenge that Job could have understood this concept from the mere routine of burnt offerings. Job had a revelation from God, and this was part of his uniqueness and explains further why there were, "None like Him in the earth."

Job knew that he had a redeemer and that He was alive. Job also was somehow aware that Jesus (the Redeemer Job was referencing) would be standing here on the Earth in the latter days. This puts Christ here, and in a position of authority. Sounds like Job had a revelation of the "Millennial reign of Christ."

I do believe we can receive revelation, but I don't believe in "extra-biblical revelation such as through other so-called holy books, dreams and visions, visits to heaven or hell, or new revelation that comes from self-appointed so-called prophets and apostles. The idea that these are equal to Scripture is ludicrous, which I totally reject.

The Bible is the revealed Word of God. It is not outdated and it does not need any help from us or some new oracle. I believe that God gives dreams and visions, and it is possible that people have actually visited Heaven or Hell. I do not believe that people visiting Heaven or Hell can "add" anything to revealed Scripture as we have it today. We know that the Apostle Paul visited Heaven, but was not permitted to describe anything about his visit there. If

Paul could not say anything about his visit there, why is it that the rules have now changed?

When you investigate different claims of heavenly visits, you will notice many discrepancies in their stories, and there are also numerous differences in their descriptions of what they actually see. There is absolutely no uniformity in their visitational claims, and if there is, such is not found in Scripture: like a "tunnel," or a light, or relatives and friends greeting them.

I said all of that to demonstrate that Job received a true revelation from God. If we are to receive a revelation from God, we will find it in His Word, not from some angel or other experience. Mohammed received his revelations for the Koran from an angel claiming to be "Gabriel." Joseph Smith (founder of the Mormon church) received his book of Mormon from a so-called angel named "Moroni."

There is no new revelation. A revelation may be "new" to you or me, but it was in God's Word all along until we actually saw or discovered it for ourselves, or until the Holy Spirit revealed it to us.

When people claim that there are rooms in Heaven with extra "body parts" and new organs for us and acres and acres of antique cars that God had waiting for our grandparents and others of generations past who didn't have enough faith to receive them, I have to draw the line. Such "revelation" is total garbage, not biblical, being totally erroneous and useless.

Job had a revelation of Jesus Christ! Job also had faith as he continued with his revelation in chapter 19: **Job 19:25-26,** "For I know *that* my redeemer liveth, and *that* He shall stand at the latter *day* upon the earth: **26** And *though* after my skin *worms* destroy this *body,* yet in my flesh shall I see God."

Wow! Now that is revelation. How could Job know this if it had not been revealed to him by the Holy Spirit? This explains why Job was perfect in his approach to serving God. All that was required of him by God is what he did, plus, he had faith.

Remember what Jesus said after His resurrection in: **Luke 24:39,** "Behold my hands and my feet, that it is I myself: handle me, and see; for a spirit hath not flesh and bones, as ye see me have."

Jesus was in his glorified body when He made this statement. How could Job know these facts? It is such dialogue as this which proves the Book of Job to be divinely inspired. Job truly was a real personage who had real experiences. Apparently, Job had a relationship with God and did know his redeemer since God was revealing prophetic insight to him!

Remember how the Passover sacrifice "covered" and protected all who were inside the blood covering? As God said: "When I see the blood, I will pass over you."

God has respect for blood. We know also that blood has a voice. Remember what God told Cain after he had slain his brother Abel? **Genesis 4:10,** "And He said, What hast thou done? The voice of thy brother's blood crieth unto me from the ground."

We also have from the writer of Hebrews this account in **Hebrews 12:24,** "And to Jesus the mediator of the new covenant, and to the blood of sprinkling, that speaketh better things than *that of* Abel."

Scriptures such as these can be enigmatic in their construct if we fail to perceive the power of the blood. There "is" power in the blood, as Lewis E. Jones penned this song in 1899 must have known. I am told, and it is my understanding, he was also a classmate of the renowned evangelist, Billy Sunday.

God told the Israelites on the eve of Passover: "When I see the blood, I will pass over you." The Passover was similar in many ways to Job's experience. It was the blood that protected Israel from the death angel, and I believe it was blood that gave Job his protection. We should not forget that the Passover did not happen until after the Book of Job was written. Job did not have a Passover, but he did have a "hedge of protection." Where did the hedge come from if not from the blood covering that Job was continually shedding? The symbolism is the same.

Why wouldn't God protect Job with blood? The Passover itself depended on a blood covering over the home. Job as high priest of his family covered all the family's sins everyday with blood. Thusly, Job and his family were constantly covered in blood. The standard of blood was what God required to cover sins and atone for them.

Job would daily "sanctify" his sons and daughters. How could he do this? We know that he did. **Job 1:5,** "And it was so, when

The Gospel According to Job

the days of *their* feasting were gone about, that Job sent and sanctified them, and rose up early in the morning, . ."

Next, Job rose up early in the morning and offered burnt offerings for his sons and daughters. Job rose early and sacrificed early to prevent the enemy from mounting an attack against him. Job always wanted to get an early start as he was uncomfortable with the idea of having sins in his family that had not yet been atoned for. It was behavior such as this that constituted Job's demeanor as being "perfect" and upright. He never wasted any time when it came to being in a righteous state before God. I would wish that the church of today would be so attentive.

We can't place too much emphasis on the fact that Job always rose early to sacrifice. This was so key to his God given protection. If you will take notice of this fact, you will realize that this provided Job and his family with an almost constant flow of blood to cover his family. He would start early in the morning every day. "Thus did Job continually." Remember that continually really means continually. It was a continuous daily process.

Everything that Job did was in accordance with: Hebrews 9:22, "And almost all things are by the law purged with blood; and without shedding of blood is no remission."

An important fact we cannot overlook is that without the shedding of blood, there can be no remission for sin. Again, Adam and Eve's fig leaves were not suitable or acceptable to God to cover them. Something had to be slain, and blood had to be shed to cover their sins, and might I suggest that the animal slain for their sin could possibly have been a lamb?

Job was in a constant state of shedding sacrificial blood for sins. Scripture explains to us that sins cannot be remitted (the release from the sin penalty paid) or that the sin being covered or taken away will not happen without a blood sacrifice. May I also remind you that the sacrifices of Job merely "covered" sin, while the finished work on the cross by Jesus Christ "takes our sin away."

John 1:29, "The next day John seeth Jesus coming unto Him, and saith, 'Behold the Lamb of God, which taketh away the sin of the world.'"

Somehow Job knew that God required blood to remit sins. Did he know this from the patriarchs and their examples? I don't really know how he knew, or where he got his information, but he most certainly did know. I would say again, that the ancient customs of his day would have required that he would know the oral traditions handed down from such ancestors as Abraham, Isaac, and Jacob. That is how it was done in those days. Job in turn would have passed these traditions down to his sons. During this historical time period, it was Job's duty as the high priest of his family to offer the sacrifices for his entire family household.

Throughout all of this, we can't forget that Satan has been on his quest to try and find out how and where he can gain access to Job and to his family. Satan has been relentless.

The Gospel According to Job

Satan was watching Job very closely as God had commanded him. He knew Job was continually sacrificing blood. He probably had "around the clock" surveillance of Job and all of his activities. Job was unaware he was under Satan's microscope. Job simply went about his daily business of sacrificing his burnt offerings to God without knowing his every move was being scrutinized by the enemy of his soul.

By this point Satan was obsessed with just getting his hands on Job or his family. If he could only steal, kill, and destroy! Satan was totally driven to penetrate the hedge of protection God had constructed and placed around Job. He would not give up! He wouldn't quit. He was determined to find his access to Job no matter what it would take. After all, God had indicated to him that all Job had was in his power and available.

As we stated before, it appears that Satan had never encountered such a hedge anytime previously prior to his experiences and interactions with Job. Satan needed to know how this hedge got there and how he could prevent it from coming back. We have to be able to discern that whatever this hedge was, and whatever it was made of was apparently too strong for Satan to breach. Hence, Satan's complaints concering it. For some reason, Satan could not find even one point of entry through it, no matter how resourceful he was.

This once again brings us to: Job 1:13, "(<u>And there was a day when</u>) his sons and his daughters were eating and drinking wine in their eldest brother's house."

Yes, as mentioned before, this was the day.

This was the day Satan had been waiting for all along. He finally figured it out. He saw how to get his access. He saw it. It was now very plain. Why couldn't he have seen this before? It was there all the time. Satan made the same mistake that we sometimes do, that being: "dismissal of the obvious." The old proverb is correct that we, "sometimes can't see the forest for the trees."

"And there was a day (when)." Satan realized that Job's sons and daughters were presently drinking and feasting right now, even at this very moment! Satan knows that he cannot cross the bloodline. However, the most recent sins of Job's sons were in the process of being committed right now. Job's sons and daughters were eating and drinking in their eldest brothers' house at this very moment. The ramifications of this insight are enormous. Satan now realized he had to attack Job and his family (before) his son's sins could be atoned for! If Satan would attack Job and his family right now, he could get through the hedge since these present sins had not been atoned for! No blood had yet been applied to these sins!

Let us not forget the time and day Job lived in. There wasn't any Bible scripture or Ten Commandments, etc. No law. There was only sacrifice. If Satan could attack right now prior to the daily and early morning sacrifices of Job, he could prevail. Job will not be able to get up early enough to atone for these sins that are now in progress, which his sons and daughters are committing at this very moment.

Satan realized and he knew once these sins had been atoned for that the hedge would be back in place and once more he would not have any access. Satan now understood that it was the blood covering that Job forever was covering his family with that constructed the hedge he could not penetrate. He understood that it was the bloodline that he could not cross.

Satan is now overjoyed and ecstatic about his chances to penetrate the hedge once and for all time. Therefore, he finally realized he must strike before any blood could be shed to cover the sins of Job's children. The attack had to come "<u>during</u>" the feasting and prior to any blood sacrifices to cover these sins. Aren't you glad it doesn't work this way today?

Satan finally found his access to breach the hedge around Job, so he hit Job's family and he hit them hard! We can't forget God's instructions to Satan when He sent him off to do his case study of Job. God told Satan this: **Job 1:12,** "And the Lord said unto Satan, 'Behold, all that he hath *is* in thy power; only upon himself put not forth thine hand.' So Satan went forth from the presence of the Lord."

Satan surely understood the terms of the agreement with God. Even though it was his desire to penetrate the hedge to have access to Job and do him harm, he agreed and knew he was not allowed to harm Job personally or bodily. Just discovering how to gain access to Job was not enough to personally harm him. With this in mind, remember he is not yet allowed to harm Job himself.

At this point, just before we see what Satan does now that he finally has access, it is necessary to demonstrate a valid point, and the reason for something God did when He gave Moses the law. This will help to demonstrate and to clarify the position Job was in.

Because of the long life of Job and the time of his trial, this can be of great importance. We do not know these time frames exactly, but they can be estimated from other events. Job is believed to have been around 70 years old at the time of his trial. Job 42:16-17 says this concerning Job's death: "After this lived Job an hundred and forty years, and saw his sons, and his sons' sons, *even* four generations. **17** So Job died, *being* old and full of days."

If we look at the time of the birth of Job's father Issachar, we would suppose that Job died 10-20 years before Moses brought the children of Israel out of Egypt. We also have previously mentioned that Satan apparently never had encountered such a hedge of protection before his ordeal with Job. We will need to take a look for a moment at certain portions of the Law of Moses and in particular the area of sacrifices.

Chapter Nine

The Daily Sacrifice

Moses through the Law instituted what was known as the "daily sacrifice." The daily sacrifice was known as an appeasement and communication offering to God. It was the daily sacrifice. This sacrifice was considered as the foundational sacrifice, which came first every day, and only after it could any other sacrifices be made. This offering symbolized the beginning and the ending of each day. It was a continuous offering that never stopped. It is sometimes called: "tamid," which means perpetual, continuous, always, and uninterrupted. The daily offering was a continual sacrifice.

The daily sacrifice was a symbol of the blood of Christ and the fire was never to go out. Never. It was the daily sacrifice that initiated everything else the priests would do and all other work that pertained to the sanctuary. If it were not for the daily sacrifice, there could be no offering for sin, as the sin offering followed the daily sacrifice. If there was no daily sacrifice, there could not be an offering on the Day of Atonement either. The daily sacrifice was what activated the normal sanctuary daily program. Without it, nothing else could take place.

Now let us look at what Moses instituted.

Exodus 29:38, "Now this *is that* which thou shalt offer upon the altar; two lambs of the first year day by day continually."

We now have established that every day will begin with the sacrifice of two lambs of the first year. This is to be carried out every day, and it is to be continuous. It is to never stop.

Exodus 29:39, "The one lamb thou shalt offer in the morning; and the other lamb thou shalt offer at evening." These instructions are quite clear and precise. One of the two lambs will be offered in the morning, while the other will be offered in the evening each day. The day is divided into two periods of 12 hours each.

Exodus 29:42, "This shall be a continual burnt offering throughout your generations at the door of the tabernacle of the congregation before the Lord: where I will meet you, to speak there unto thee."

This was a literal constant sacrifice. It never stopped by command of God.

Can you imagine why God instituted a daily sacrifice, which initiated all others by which He commanded that it was always to burn perpetually and never to go out? I think I can. I think God initiated such a sacrifice to keep Satan from doing to the children of Israel what he did to Job. If the sacrifice began in the morning and eventually ended in the evening by another evening sacrifice, Satan could not make any attacks "before" an atonement could be made. When you realize that no other sacrifices could be made until after the daily sacrifice had been offered, we see what God was doing. Once the evening sacrifice was over, the morning sacrifice was repeated. This cycle never stopped.

As any student of Scripture or Bible prophecy will explain, Antiochus Epiphanes was what we understand as a "type of the antichrist." In other words he symbolized the antichrist in the Old Testament by his actions. What exactly was it that Antiochus Epiphanes did? To find out we must go to:

Daniel 11:31: "And arms shall stand on his part, and they shall pollute the sanctuary of strength, and shall take away the daily *sacrifice*, and they shall place the abomination that maketh desolate."

I don't have time to go into all the sacrifices and their details, but you can be sure that Jesus Christ was depicted or symbolized in each of them. When we understand the gravity of this, we can begin to see how important the daily sacrifice had become to Israel. You could not begin a day without it! Can we live a moment without Christ? Would anyone want to? How can you start a day or anything else without Christ? Nothing is more important! Jesus Christ is "The Beginning and the End!"

Antiochus Epiphanes actually means: God manifest, as He claimed Diety. When He entered Jerusalem, He did the following as recorded by Daniel:

Daniel 8:11, "Yea, He magnified *himself* even to the prince of the host, and by Him the daily *sacrifice* was taken away, and the place of his sanctuary was cast down."

Antiochus Epiphanes is famous for stopping the daily sacrifices, which by definition caused all other sacrifices to cease, and then he proceeded to sacrifice an unclean animal, specifically a pig, upon the altar. He also commanded the worship of Zeus.

I understand that the Maccabees are not canonical scripture, but they do give an accurate historical account of these events.

2 Maccabees 5:11–14, "Says this about Antiochus Epiphanes: When these happenings were reported to the king, he thought that Judea was in revolt. Raging like a wild animal, he set out from Egypt and took Jerusalem by storm. He ordered his soldiers to cut down without mercy those whom they met and to slay those who took refuge in their houses. There was a massacre of young and old, a killing of women and children, a slaughter of virgins and infants. In the space of three days, eighty thousand were lost, forty thousand meeting a violent death, and the same number being sold into slavery."

Daniel also addresses the Antichrist. Let's look to see what Daniel says the Antichrist does at the halfway point of the tribulation.

Daniel 12:11, "And from the time *that* the daily *sacrifice* shall be taken away, and the abomination that maketh desolate set up, *there shall be* a thousand two hundred and ninety days."

We understand this act to be made by the Antichrist in the newly rebuilt temple that is soon to be constructed in Israel. Daily sacrifices will have at this time been reinstituted at the 3rd temple. Again, the daily sacrifice is taken away which dictates that there can be virtually no more sacrifices made. This act in itself is the defining exploit of the Antichrist, which initiates the second half of the tribulation and plunges planet Earth into the "Great Tribulation."

I think it is rather interesting to know that the forerunner of the Antichrist and the type and shadow, which symbolized the Antichrist in the Old Testament, stops the daily sacrifice and desecrates the temple. While the New Testament records that this is precisely what the Antichrist will do when he takes control of Jerusalem at which time he sets himself up as God in the Temple.

Matthew 24:15-16, "When ye therefore shall see the abomination of desolation, spoken of by Daniel the prophet, stand in the holy place, (whoso readeth, let him understand:) **16** Then let them which be in Judaea flee into the mountains." We have this scripture spoken by Jesus telling us of the Antichrist making the new 3rd Jewish temple desolate.

We have this scripture showing us its fulfillment: **2 Thessalonians 2:4,** "Who opposeth and exalteth himself above all that is called God, or that is worshipped; so that he as God sitteth in the temple of God, shewing himself that he is God."

When Satan discovered he could penetrate the hedge surrounding Job that was something that could have drastic ramifications for the rest of Israel and the world. But when God instituted the law of Moses, He took away Satan's ability to attack someone before the sin he committed could be atoned for, but this was not the case with Job. Even today, you can still hear someone say: "You need to get that under the blood," although this does not occur as often as it once did.

Now we come to a very interesting and illuminating discourse of events. Satan has shown us much about himself throughout this entire ordeal with Job than I believe that he ever intended. We generally don't think in terms of Satan's weaknesses, but maybe we should. It is a fact that he surely takes advantage of ours!

Many of us have made mistakes in our lives that we truly regret, but in retrospect of those mistakes we can surely see the hand that Satan had in our making of those mistakes. We didn't just get out of bed on a certain day and decide we would make one of the worst decisions of our life.

We just can't forget that as we mentioned in the beginning of this discourse that there is a constant battle raging in the spirit world. The forces of God and Satan's emissaries are constantly at war, literally. We as human beings are stuck right in the middle of that war. The truth be known, the war between heavenly angels and Satan's demonic hordes is being waged because of us. I understand that we are not the center of the universe, and I also concede that there is more to the picture than just God and Satan at war because of the race of man. But, much of the eternal struggle between right and wrong concerns mankind and their decisions.

Just look at the ramifications of the decision Abraham made to go into Hagar and conceive Ishmael. It is quite obvious that he didn't consult with God prior to that decision. We are still living with the after effects of that major blunder today after about 4000 years or so.

Today, Ishmael is Islam. I understand Esau, Moab, and others are as well, but we can see that the decisions made by these early players in the human drama have had lasting negative effects that are still relevant in today's world.

It is just so easy to think that what we do is insignificant when the opposite is true. Our very souls and eternal existence may be decided on a single spiritual battle that is lost. I could give many examples, but I don't want to prolong anything. I would expect that just the mentioning of the name of one "Judas Iscariot" would be sufficient. Jesus said of him in: **Matthew 26:24,** "The Son of man goeth as it is written of Him: but woe unto that man by whom the Son of man is betrayed! It had been good for that man if he had not been born."

Every time I read that scripture, I get chills up and down my spine. What a statement! As we well know, Judas wasn't forced to betray Jesus, for all the wrong reasons it just seemed to him as the right thing to do at the time. How much more wrong could he have been. It certainly appears that once Judas had seen the course of events that followed his betrayal of Christ, he tried to reverse the process by returning the thirty pieces of silver. Of course we know this was not effective, and Jesus was crucified and Judas went out and hanged himself. For Jesus to say that it would have been good for Judas to have never been born is mind blowing to me.

My point is this, we should not make any major decisions in life without praying about them and asking for God's guidance. As long as we have a witness in our spirit that what we decide is in the will of God, we can have peace about it. I am sure that we have all heard about God's permissive will and His perfect will. I am not going to investigate that specific theological debate, but I think you can see my point. The decisions that Job made were "life" decisions and they governed his entire lifespan.

Why would we be any different? The decisions we make today may affect our eternal habitation. We simply need to remind ourselves of this because the eternal war is still in full swing and it will not let up until Satan is finally cast into the lake of fire (which just happens to be one of my very favorite scriptures)

Revelation 20:10, "And the devil that deceived them was cast into the lake of fire and brimstone, where the beast and the false prophet *are*, and shall be tormented day and night for ever and ever."

I like to quote this scripture to Satan from time to time just to remind him of what his future is. I'm sure he appreciates it.

Chapter Ten

Loss of the Hedge

But now, we have Satan about to pounce on Job and his family as he has figured out the system. However, it is necessary and of the utmost importance that we notice Satan's strategy to engage into the battle against Job. Through the attack upon Job, Satan actually will reveal what he fears most. I just hope I can show it to you plainly. Once understood, it is very powerful indeed.

When Satan found his access, he still did not attack Job personally! The first reason was that God had previously told Satan: "All that he hath is in thy power, only upon himself put not forth thine hand." Satan was still not allowed to touch Job. He could only touch the things Job had. God was very specific in His speech when He said that all Job had was in Satan's power. In other words, the hedge was down, but Job was off limits and untouchable. Satan would be restricted to only those things Job owned or possessed. Besides, it was not Job that was engaged in the acts of drinking and eating in his oldest sons' house. And we can be most certain that Job was not involved in cursing God in any way. Job was not at fault here; it was his children that were involved in their less than perfect behavior.

How long had Satan waited for this moment! How many times had he thought about what he would do to Job once he could penetrate through the hedge. This was a dream come true for him. Now he could finally fulfill his mission against Job and steal, kill, and destroy everything belonging to him. All this time it had been Job that was marked with a big target on his back. After all, Job was Satan's ultimate objective. It was Job that Satan wanted most. Satan is ready to unleash all the forces of evil he has in his arsenal and direct them straight at Job in one fast wave of destruction. Everything Job had worked for all of his life is in the path of Satan for total annihilation. There is no stopping Satan now. The hedge of protection is down and all the forces of the damned are present to claim Job's territory for the army of Satan.

Once more I would remind everyone that Satan's objective has always been to destroy Job. And you would think that with the hedge being down Satan would march directly through and attack Job himself. But this is not what Satan did because he couldn't.

The hedge is down. Surely Satan can now destroy Job once and for all, right? No he can't, and he bypasses attacks on Job to get to his family. Let's now look at the course of events that Satan utilized against Job. When thinking this through, we must understand that Satan has no doubt formulated a "plan of attack" in which he can ultimately achieve his objective against Job. Since he now knows "How the System Works," he is prepared.

Job 1:14, "And there came a messenger unto Job, and said, 'The oxen were plowing, and the asses feeding beside them." This messenger no doubt was running and out of breath as he informed Job that there was a problem with the oxen and the donkeys that were with them.

When Job heard this, he immediately knew an attack was in progress as he may have started to imagine a plan of defense to extract any thieves or other dangerous elements from his property. Remember, that Satan steals, is a thief, and comes to destroy.

Job's messenger continued with his story in verse 15: "And the Sabeans fell *upon them,* and took them away; yea, they have slain the servants with the edge of the sword; and I only am escaped alone to tell thee."

It is imperative we witness the entire scope of events that is in progress here. Again, Satan is not attacking Job personally, even though Job is the ultimate objective. Instead, we are informed that the Sabeans have slain Job's servants with the sword and have taken away his oxen and his donkeys.

At this point, allow me to just make a small conjectural surmising. Could it be possible there is a hidden prophetic event here that we can see being played out right now? Something that has been in the works for a long time? Here we have a righteous Israelite of the tribe of Issachar. His servants are attacked by a group of Sabeans wielding the "edge of the sword." It just so happens the ancient Sabeans were the principal people of Saudi Arabia in ancient times. I ask you if there are those wielding swords today who want to destroy everything the righteous Jewish people have? Has much changed since Job's day? Exactly what is the relationship today with the Jews in Israel and the principal people of Saudi Arabia? It is my understanding to this day, and at the time of this writing, it is illegal for a person of Jewish descent to even enter the borders of Saudi Arabia.

This latest news Job receives is devastating to say the least. His trusted servants that watched over his oxen and his donkeys have been murdered. Furthermore, the oxen and donkeys have been stolen by these killers. It doesn't stop here, there is more.

Job 1:16, "While he *was* yet speaking, there came also another, and said, 'The fire of God is fallen from heaven, and hath burned up the sheep, and the servants, and consumed them; and I only am escaped alone to tell thee.'"

Now Job is confronted with more tragic news. While the initial messenger was still relating the tragedy of the oxen and donkeys being stolen and the murder of his trusted servants, a second messenger arrives. This servant or messenger mentions that the fire of God has fallen from Heaven. First of all, I seriously doubt that this fire was from God. It is quite doubtful that this messenger understood what was going on, and even to this day, whenever any type of "natural" disaster occurs, we continue to call such an event "an act of God." I am not trying to make scripture into what I want it to say, but this sounds like it could have possibly been an electrical storm with bolts of lightning, which was directed by the "prince and power of the air." If you remember when Jesus was on Earth, He rebuked dangerous winds and said: "Peace, be still." It is in this sense we need to understand this messenger's statement. It is quite doubtful this messenger could accurately discern the origin of this fire. Since this fire happened very quickly after the hedge had been breached, I think we can rest assured who was behind it.

The result of this fire was that all of Job's sheep were burned up in an instant. Totally destroyed with none left. When you think of the astronomical number of sheep Job had, this must have been quite a thunderbolt! Scripture declares that Job received double his blessing after his encounter and trial. He was rewarded with 14,000 sheep at the end, which means this thunderbolt destroyed 7,000 sheep.

Not only does Job lose all of his sheep, he also lost all of the shepherds he had as servants who watched over them. Job has now lost all of his cattle, donkeys, and sheep. He has also lost all of his servants that cared for them. We know that Job must have had 500 oxen and 500 female donkeys among his herds. He truly was the richest man in the country. But now, they were all gone - in one day!

And if that was not enough, let's look at verse 17:

Job 1:17, "While he *was* yet speaking, there came also another, and said, 'The Chaldeans made out three bands, and fell upon the camels, and have carried them away, yea, and slain the servants with the edge of the sword; and I only am escaped alone to tell thee.' "

Now comes the final nail in the coffin. One last messenger arrives to tell Job that the Chaldeans had come and started carrying off his camels and took them all away. And one last time, all the servants caring for the camels were also murdered. In each message, only the messenger was left alive, everyone else was killed. We also know that Job had 3,000 camels that were stolen.

In review, Job had seven thousand sheep destroyed. There was the loss of five hundred oxen, and five hundred female donkeys or she asses. Three thousand camels were also stolen. This is a total of eleven thousand head of livestock and camels either stolen or killed in one day and in a matter of minutes.

Everything Job had when he woke up that morning was now gone in an instant. When I said that Satan hit Job and his family hard, that was an understatement. Besides all of this, all of his shepherds, servants, and workers except for three individuals have all been murdered.

The hedge had been penetrated in one single day, and probably in less than an hour; everything Job owned was gone, totally gone. Job's entire lifetime's worth of work up in smoke, literally. Things could just not have been any worse.

At this point in time allow me to make an observation. This is the point that demonstrates to us what Satan fears most. Satan actually reveals to us his greatest fear by the chain of events that he has undertaken in his attacks upon Job.

The Gospel According to Job

Let's do a quick review of the events.

Job 1:14, "And there came a messenger unto Job, and said, 'The oxen were plowing, and the asses feeding beside them."

Job 1:15, "And the Sabeans fell *upon them*, and took them away; yea, they have slain the servants with the edge of the sword; and I only am escaped alone to tell thee." This was the very first attack against Job.

Job 1:16, "While he *was* yet speaking, there came also another, and said, the fire of God is fallen from heaven, and hath burned up the sheep, and the servants, and consumed them; and I only am escaped alone to tell thee." This was the second recorded attack against Job.

The question must be asked: "If Satan wanted to attack Job so badly, why does he begin with oxen, and sheep?" Certainly Satan did not feel challenged by Job's livestock? Or did he? Satan has just shown us how much of a coward he is while he demonstrates what he fears most. The reason Satan did not attack Job or his family was because he knew he must first remove the BLOOD SOURCE!

After all, these were the animals that Job used to make his blood sacrifices and offerings. Satan knew that he would not be able to harm Job or his family unless this source was totally removed from the battlefield. Satan knew and understood that Job's wealth and "All that he hath" was not restricted to only his sacrificial animals!

Satan understood that if he was going to inflict harm to Job or his family, he had to first remove the blood. This was the hedge creating blood. The blood that symbolized the blood of Jesus. The atoning blood. The sin covering blood. The power of the blood had to be removed before Satan could kill, steal, and destroy Job or his family!

Satan's strategy worked. He totally understood what had to be done, and he did it. Remove the blood source! Get the blood out of the way first! Satan realized if he didn't remove the blood source immediately, that Job would just rise early the next day and make a blood atonement for his children and the hedge would be back in place and he would be locked out once more having no access. Next, the servants were all slain which meant Job had nobody to help to perform the duties needed to make all the sacrifices.

Today, we seem to forget all that is involved in offering so many sacrifices. Job had ten children. Can you imagine the manpower it took to sacrifice ten bullocks or sheep in one day? This was a massive undertaking, and Job needed his servants help to carry out the ordeal and all the details of that many blood offerings. Job simply couldn't do it all by himself.

And last but not least, the donkeys and camels were all stolen. You may think this is insignificant since neither of these animals were ever used in blood sacrifices. Well, you would be correct in your logic, but without any camels or donkeys, none of the needed materials for offerings could be procured.

The Gospel According to Job

Who could carry all the necessary wood needed for the fires? What about all the other materials that would be necessary? How would such material be transported to the sacrifice areas? How would the servants and Job travel? What about the altars themselves, did they need repair, or were they even built? Did each altar burn up with the sacrifice? We don't know all the answers to these questions, but we do know that without any donkeys or camels it was impossible to travel anywhere to procure anything that pertained to a blood offering. Job could not even travel or go anywhere to even try to purchase an animal to sacrifice. Besides, with no livestock, he had nothing to use for money.

Now for the bad news. If you thought things could not get any worse, Job's disaster has now just turned into a once in a lifetime total catastrophe of complete ruination.

Job 1:18, "While he *was* yet speaking, there came also another, and said, thy sons and thy daughters *were* eating and drinking wine in their eldest brother's house."

Can you imagine what went through Job's mind at this point? The first three messengers brought tragic news about his sheep, his oxen, his donkeys, and his camels. Not to mention that all of his servants had been killed! I am certain that Job loved many of them and you know that he would have treated them well. There is no doubt they were loyal and faithful to him.

Now we have a messenger that mentions Job's sons and daughters that were eating and drinking wine in their eldest brother's house. As I mentioned before, Satan attacked them during their feasting and while it was in progress. This was the only way Satan could gain access through the hedge. He designed a plan and executed it flawlessly.

Now Job is in a position where he has no blood source remaining for any sacrifices. Satan now has the upper hand and he is going in for the kill!

Job 1:19, "And, behold, there came a great wind from the wilderness, and smote the four corners of the house, and it fell upon the young men, and they are dead; and I only am escaped alone to tell thee."

Now we have a weather related incident that sounds like it could have been straight-line winds, a tornado, windstorm, or some other type of meteorological disaster. This definitely was not an act of God. On the contrary, we know who was behind it. This storm or whatever it was truly was catastrophic as it killed all of Job's children who were celebrating and drinking wine in the destroyed home of the oldest brother. What a tragedy. What a day!

Chapter Eleven

The Woven Thread

All of this occurred because of one thing. Satan stopped the "CYCLE OF BLOOD" that was used to create Job's hedge of protection. By stopping the cycle of blood, Satan was able to gain access to Job's family. Job had no "Covering" at this point and was helpless against the onslaught.

Here it is all summed up in one paragraph:

We noticed in verse 19 this equation: Now that the oxen are all gone, and now that the sheep are all dead, and Job has no more animals for blood sacrifice, and all sources of transporting sacrifices to the altar have been destroyed with NO SOURCE of blood remaining; only then is Job's family attacked and killed! Satan could do nothing until the blood source was gone! This my friend, is how the system works. It is all about the blood. This is a picture of the gospel on the first page and in the first chapter of scripture! This demonstrates to us that the very first chapter of written scripture is: "ALL ABOUT THE BLOOD!"

This is why it is so important that our churches return to the "gospel" of Jesus Christ and abandon the "bloodless" gospel that they have picked up along the way to increase the size of their congregations. What good is a megachurch of 30,000 where everyone is motivated and happy, if no one is covered in the blood of Jesus?

Today there is a vast difference with what happened to Job, and what we can do. Job only had symbolic blood of animals that represented Jesus' sacrifice on the cross. Today, we have the actual blood of Jesus that can be applied to you personally! Satan can't take that away, and he certainly won't try to cross such a bloodline! We sometimes forget just how powerful the blood of Jesus Christ is. Do not underestimate the blood of Jesus. Satan can no longer remove the blood source, he cannot cross the bloodline; he is defeated by the blood! Praise the name of the Lord!

Something we need to know, if Satan is to gain access to you now, he must go back to what he first did in Genesis chapter 3 with Eve, and tempt his way inside the hedge. We must not forget that Adam and Eve themselves in the beginning were: Untouchable! Before there was sin in their lives and prior to their receiving a "Sin Nature," Satan could not touch them either!

Satan now gains access from "inside" the hedge. This means we give him his access to us as he cannot cross the bloodline to get inside. When we yield to his temptations, a breach occurs in the hedge.

I also understand we are subject to the aging process and there are results from growing old, but that is not what I am speaking of here since we will all die as a result of something if we pass on prior to the rapture. However, healing for our bodies has been included for us through Christ's shed blood. By His stripes we are healed and were healed.

Allow me to begin to close this exercise with a small addendum. The entire story of Job chapter 1 has definite prophetic implications. As you know, I am a student of Bible prophecy; so, let me explain how the Pre-Tribulational Rapture of the Church is found in Job chapter 1.

Satan and the Antichrist want total control of the Earth. During the period known to us as the Tribulation, they will indeed take huge control.

2 Thessalonians 2:7, "For the mystery of iniquity doth already work: only he who now letteth *will let*, until he be taken out of the way."

I have always used the King James Version Bible and I always will. But, we do not use the word "let" in the same manner in which the King James translators used it in the 1600's. The word "let" here literally means to "restrain." The NIV says it this way:

"For the secret power of lawlessness is already at work; but the one who now holds it back will continue to do so till he is taken out of the way."

The NASB says it this way: [7]

"For the mystery of lawlessness is already at work; only <u>he who now restrains</u> *will do so* until he is taken out of the way."

I could go on with these examples, but I think you get the picture.

Beginning with 2nd Thessalonians chapter 2, we are introduced to the context of verse number 7 quoted previously.

2 Thessalonians 2:1 says: "Now we beseech you, brethren, by the coming of our Lord Jesus Christ, and *by* our gathering together unto Him, . . ."

The coming of our Lord Jesus Christ and our gathering together unto Him is most definitely the context here and we have a definite reference to the rapture of the Church. There may be a reference to the Second Coming here in the first half of the verse, (as some Theologians suggest), but there is certainly a mentioning of a "gathering together" at the rapture. I am not going to get into that debate here, but the rapture is a common theme in 1st and 2nd Thessalonians. The context is about the rapture or a "gathering together unto Him."

2 Thessalonians 2:3, "Let no man deceive you by any means: for *that day shall not come*, except there come a falling away first, and that man of sin be revealed, the son of perdition;" Paul is now explaining that there will be an apostasy and departing from truth within the church, and then the Antichrist will be revealed. Some actually teach that this departing is the (Departure) of the Church itself in the rapture.

2 Thessalonians 2:4, "Who opposeth and exalteth himself above all that is called God, or that is worshipped; so that he as God sitteth in the temple of God, shewing himself that he is God." For this reason we know this is the Antichrist being referenced here as Jesus described this exact situation in: **Matthew 24:15-16,** "When ye therefore shall see the abomination of desolation, spoken of by Daniel the prophet, stand in the holy place, (whoso readeth, let him understand:) **16** Then let them which be in Judaea flee into the mountains."

I understand that the Holy Spirit resides on Earth within the true church of Jesus Christ. There is no doubt about this. We now go to the words of Jesus in: **John 14:17,** "*Even* the Spirit of truth; whom the world cannot receive, because it seeth Him not, neither knoweth Him: but ye know Him; for He dwelleth with you, and shall be in you." (Notice, "he" shall be in you!)

After Pentecost, the Holy Spirit came and dwelt within the Church, and he has remained there ever since. The work the Holy Spirit does, He does within the Church on Earth. After all, the church is "the Body of Christ."

Romans 8:11, "But if the Spirit of Him that raised up Jesus from the dead dwell in you, He that raised up Christ from the dead shall also quicken your mortal bodies by his Spirit that dwelleth in you." The Holy Spirit surely dwells within the Church. That is where He resides. I certainly would not want to live a single day without his indwelling presence. If you are a Christian, you understand what I am saying.

2 Thessalonians 2:7, "For the mystery of iniquity doth already work: only he who now letteth *will let*, until he be taken out of the way." Again, he who now restrains will restrain until he is taken out of the way. This is obviously a reference to the Body of Christ on the Earth being removed at the rapture of the church. Allow me to demonstrate.

1 Corinthians 12:27, "Now ye are the body of Christ, and members in particular. (The body of Christ is a "he,") and the Holy Spirit is a "He," who dwells inside the true church of Jesus Christ. These are well understood Bible Truths. Such truths simply need to be put in the proper prophetic perspective.

For those of you who are not Pre-Tribulation rapture believers, you may not like this, but it is quite plain. No one is teaching that the Church will not know tribulation or persecution. On the contrary, I believe we will experience a surge of both in the coming days before the rapture. However, there is a huge difference in tribulations and persecutions, when compared to the Great Tribulation. There is also a monumental difference between man's wrath and God's wrath (which is the tribulational wrath as described in the Book of Revelation.)

We, as the Church, are too powerful for the Antichrist to come to power. We are the Body of Christ. Right? We are the earthly home of the Holy Spirit, as He dwells and works through us, His Church. Right? Satan is a powerful being, but the Antichrist will not come to power until the Church (indwelt by the Holy Spirit) that is restraining him is removed. There is a very good reason for this and it explains why the Two Witnesses are here during the Tribulation and the 144,000 are witnessing about Christ. "The Church isn't here to do it!"

After all, it was the mandate of the Church to make disciples and go into all the world and preach the Gospel, Right?

"He who now restrains will restrain (the church) until he (the church or body of Christ) be taken out of the way" (raptured). I know we get caught up in the "Symbolism" of the Church being the "Bride of Christ." As a result we don't think in terms of the Church as a he. Well, are we, or are we not, the "Body of Christ?" We can't be Hermaphroditic!

We are truly illustrated in Scripture as the "Bride of Christ." I certainly would not deny that, as this shows the special relationship between Christ and His Church. No problem with that. However, if we ARE indwelled by the Holy Spirit, and we ARE the Body of Christ, we can't be female. Sorry, if this truth shatters your theology. (I didn't intend to go there.)

2 Thessalonians 2:8, "And then shall that Wicked be revealed, whom the Lord shall consume with the spirit of his mouth, and shall destroy with the brightness of his coming." And "Then" shall that Wicked be revealed (the Antichrist). When does this happen? After the restrainer is taken out of the way! I am not engaged in biblical gymnastics here, this is the way it reads. Once the restrainer is removed, the Antichrist comes on the scene. Go Figure.

The Church is the restrainer since the Holy Spirit within or inside of it is the force doing the restraining. This force will be removed at the rapture allowing the Antichrist to come to power without any opposition.

Just think this through logically. Isn't the Holy Spirit within the true Church of God stronger than the Antichrist? The Holy Spirit cannot be removed himself since after all, He is God. How can you remove God from anyplace? However, He lives inside the Body of Christ, and it is Him working within the church that is removed.

It's quite simple really, the Holy Spirit working inside the Church is keeping the Antichrist from appearing. But once the rapture happens, the Church is gone and the Antichrist has no forces stronger than himself left to restrain him any longer, then the world will welcome the Antichrist! Let's take a closer look.

Matthew 16:18, "And I say also unto thee, that thou art Peter, and upon this rock I will build my church; and the gates of hell shall not prevail against it."

Jesus said that the gates of Hell shall not what? I think the word was "Prevail" against His Church. Those that miss the rapture, but thought they were saved will have to regroup and prepare for a rough 7 years. With the church now gone, the force that restrained Antichrist has left the Earth. The false church left on Earth will now have to get serious with God and sad to say will probably be martyred if they do.

Many Christians think the church will go through the Tribulation. **Daniel 7:21,** "I beheld, and the same horn made war with the saints, and PREVAILED against them. The horn did what? Daniel 7:21 is happening during the height of the Tribulation and the Antichrist or "little horn," is prevailing against the Tribulation Saints. I understand there are Saints in the Tribulation that missed the rapture and subsequently get saved, but they are not "the Church." The gates of hell can't prevail against "the Church." The church has been raptured, but the Antichrist <u>is prevailing</u> against the Tribulation Saints, which also includes many Israelites that receive Jesus during the Tribulation.

Matthew 16:18, "And I say also unto thee, that thou art Peter, and upon this rock I will build my church; and the gates of hell shall not prevail against it." The Church was too strong for the Antichrist to prevail against because it was filled with the Holy Spirit. The Holy Spirit that indwells the Church and works through it must be removed prior to the arrival of the Antichrist.

1 John 4:4, "Ye are of God, little children, and have overcome them: because greater is he that is in you, than he that is in the world." This entity (the Church) must be removed before the Antichrist can come to power. The vehicle that performs this operation is what we have deemed to be the "rapture." The rapture is designed for the Church; the Tribulation is designed to bring Israel back to God and to complete Daniel's vision and prophecy of the seventy weeks. Daniel's 70th week is the Tribulation, and the seventy weeks are not a prophecy for the Church, but for: "Thy people and thy Holy City." This is speaking of the people of Daniel and the city of Jerusalem. The Church was unknown to Daniel, and the prophecy was not directed to a church, but Israel and Jerusalem. The fulfilled 69 weeks were directed to Israel, not the church, so why would the 70th week be different? By the way, the Church has not replaced Israel! That teaching is pure heresy of the highest degree!

1 Thessalonians 5:9, "For God hath not appointed us to wrath, but to obtain salvation by our Lord Jesus Christ." The wrath mentioned here is not just your typical "run of the mill" everyday wrath, but the appointed Tribulation wrath itself of which the Church by design is not meant to go through.

This now brings us to the example of the Jewish wedding feast. We can't ever forget that Jesus was Jewish, and of the tribe of Judah. The church is "symbolized as a bride" to illustrate the point of the Jewish wedding.

The people Jesus was speaking to were Jewish, and they understood the symbolism and customs He spoke of. When Jesus said; "No one knows the day or the hour wherein the Son of man cometh," this was understood already within Jewish custom. This was a reference to the Jewish wedding. Jesus was using very familiar terms and Jewish wedding customs as a symbolic idiom of Him returning for His Church.

Jesus then speaks of the ten virgins. Five were wise with oil in their lamps, and five foolish as they had no oil in their lamps at the time of the wedding procession. When Jesus said: "Only the

Father knows the time," He is making another wedding reference when the Father tells His Son to go and receive His bride and bring her to His home that He has prepared. However, the Son does not know when His Father will send Him to receive His bride (who needs to be ready at all times.)

This is what Jesus referenced when He said in: **John 14:3,** "And if I go and prepare a place for you, I will come again, and receive you unto myself; that where I am, *there* ye may be also."

Once again, Jesus was speaking of the wedding process. And by the way, He is to take us to where He is. Where is He?

Isaiah spoke of this in his picture of the rapture of the church:

Isaiah 26:19 –21, "Thy dead *men* shall live, *together with* my dead body shall they arise. Awake and sing, ye that dwell in dust: for thy dew *is as* the dew of herbs, and the earth shall cast out the dead." "My dead body arising" and then being cast out of the Earth is a reference to the rapture itself. (The dead in Christ rising.)

Next in Isaiah 26:20, this sequence is the Church again symbolized as a bride with the groom in Heaven during the indignation (Tribulation). The word "indignation" is synonymous with tribulation and is sometimes used in its place. Example:

Isaiah 34:2, "For the "indignation" of the Lord *is* upon all nations, and *his* fury upon all their armies: he hath utterly destroyed them, he hath delivered them to the slaughter." (Armageddon)

Another example is: **Daniel 11:36,** "And the king shall do according to his will; and he shall exalt himself, and magnify himself above every god, and shall speak marvelous things against the God of gods, and shall prosper till the <u>indignation be accomplished</u>: for that that is determined shall be done."

As you can see, these are not historical accounts recorded by Isaiah and Daniel, but they have a future fulfillment during the Tribulation as Daniel is referencing the Antichrist.

Finally, it all culminates with:

Isaiah 26:20, "Come, my people, enter thou into thy chambers, and shut thy doors about thee: hide thyself as it were for a little moment, until the indignation be over past." (Or, until the Tribulation is over!) In the Jewish wedding scenario, the bride and groom would close up the wedding chamber and remain inside alone for seven days since the groom came and took her to the place he had prepared.

Then after seven days, they would emerge! They were no longer twain, but one! This pictures the "Bride of Christ" being locked away with their "groom" for a period of 7 days. For Christ and the Church, it will be 7 years instead of 7 days, or the length of the Tribulation. The symbolism is unmistakable.

The Second Coming of Christ is a picture of the event when Jesus and His bride are now one and they emerge from their place after 7 years of tribulation or (indignation) have taken place on Earth and after the Marriage Supper of the Lamb has taken place in Heaven. Christ and the church are now ONE.

Completing Isaiah's account, in verse 21 we have a depiction of the Second coming right down to the destruction of those on

Earth that are trying to destroy Israel. **Isaiah 26:21,** "For, behold, the Lord cometh out of his place to punish the inhabitants of the earth for their iniquity: the earth also shall disclose her blood, and shall no more cover her slain." This is a reference to the Second coming of Christ described in Rev.19:11-16, and (fulfilled in) :

Jude 1:14-15, "And Enoch also, the seventh from Adam, prophesied of these, saying, 'Behold, the Lord cometh with ten thousands of his saints, **15** To execute judgment upon all, and to convince all that are ungodly among them of all their ungodly deeds which they have ungodly committed, and of all their hard *speeches* which ungodly sinners have spoken against him.' "

Why can't the Antichrist be revealed prior to the rapture of the church? The answer can be found in many places of Scripture, but I happen to like: **Revelation 1:5,** "And from Jesus Christ, *who is* the faithful witness, *and* the first begotten of the dead, and the prince of the kings of the earth. Unto him that loved us, and WASHED US from our sins in his own blood, ..."

IN CONCLUSION

If we, the Church, are washed by the blood of Jesus (and we are because Revelation 1:5 says we are), then this means that we have been covered by it. When you wash clothes, you drench them in the soap and water or cleaning solution. Whatever is to be cleaned must be totally submerged in the cleanser.

Our sins have been taken away by the blood of Jesus. Remember, there are only two kinds of people on Earth. Those whose sins have been washed away and those whose sins still remain. There are no other categories; there are no other options. You are either washed in the blood or you are not. You can't be partly "saved." You are part of Christ's body, or you are not.

1 John 1:7, "But if we walk in the light, as He is in the light, we have fellowship one with another, and the blood of Jesus Christ his Son cleanseth us from all sin." If anyone is saved today, this is how they got that way. There is no other way but the blood of Jesus. Our good works can't do it. Our kindness won't work either. There is nothing we can do. We could feed the world and clothe all the homeless, but it still wouldn't be enough. Only the blood of Jesus can save your soul!

1 John 3:5, "And ye know that he was manifested to take away our sins; and in him is no sin." That's how He could do it! Sinless perfection. The Holy Lamb of God. Our Savior.

We are "covered in the blood of Jesus!" We have been washed in it. When God the Father looks at us, He either sees the blood of Jesus or He doesn't. If He doesn't see blood, He sees sin.

When God looks at the redeemed, He does not see their sins. He sees blood. He sees the blood covering. God sees that we have been bought with a price as the receipt of that price is upon us. The blood of Jesus that was shed for us. After all, we have been washed in it, and drenched in it. We are literally covered in it. Praise be to God!

Chapter Twelve

The Final Conclusion

This brings us to an interesting conclusion.

If we are washed in the blood, and we are.
If we are cleansed by the blood, and we are.
If our sins are covered by the blood, and they are.
If Jesus shed his blood for me and you, and He did.
If that blood has been applied to us, and it has.
If Jesus is our Passover Lamb, and He is.
Then Jesus' blood will protect us, and it does.
If the Church is blood bought, and it is.
If the price paid for our salvation has been negotiated, and it has.

This means that since you and I are covered by the blood, Satan cannot cross that bloodline! The blood of Jesus has been applied to you and to me!

How does Jesus use His blood and where does He dispense it if not for His blood bought Church? We are bought with a price!

If it is applied, and if God can see it instead of our sins, then Satan can as well! We have the hedge! The hedge is there! It is covering you and me! The blood of Jesus! Much better than the blood Job had access to! And since this is the truth, the blood of Jesus Christ is yet in the Earth. It has been applied to the Church! Everyone that calls on Jesus and repents of their sins has access to the blood. It is available to whosoever will!

Just as Satan had to wait until all the blood source was gone before he could begin to harm Job or his family, he must wait until the Church is raptured and removed from the Earth before he can introduce the Antichrist and bring destruction to the Earth!

Why? Because of the blood that has been applied to us, that's why! Satan already showed us what he was afraid of in the Earth, and he still fears the blood of Jesus. Believe it. He will not try to take control until after that source is gone.

The blood of Jesus is the most powerful substance in the universe! It has no equal! The blood reigns supreme! It is the only substance powerful enough to remove sins. It is what Satan fears most! The blood Christ shed on Calvary destroyed everything that Satan can bring against us.

Mark 3:27, "No man can enter into a strong man's house, and spoil his goods, except he will first bind the strong man; and then he will spoil his house." How can Satan spoil the Earth while the Body of Christ is still here? Is this statement true or not: "Greater is He that is in you than he that is in the World?" Satan can't take control of the world unless he is the stronger of the two.

If you will remember, earlier in this book I mentioned that I had restless leg syndrome for twenty years, and headaches for more than forty years. I was at home sitting in my La-z-boy easy chair and I could feel an episode of restless leg coming on. I could always tell when an episode was about to begin.

This happened shortly after God had given me this understanding about Job. I sat in my chair and prayed to God something like this: "Dear God, must I suffer this violent episode?" I asked God: "Why do I have to go through this again?"

These restless leg episodes would be almost unbearable, and I didn't even know what they were back then. My toes would tense and curl up and contract, then my leg would begin to convulse uncontrollably with a feeling of a spasmodic type of a cramp and violent shaking and jerking.

Then it seemed God answered my prayer something like this. He said: "Son, what have I just revealed to you?"

At first I didn't seem to understand, but all at once I suddenly knew what to do. I immediately prayed and asked God to forgive me of all my sins. I said to God: "I know I am saved; I know I am a Christian, and I know I am filled with the Spirit. But Lord, if I have injured anyone or hurt someone that I am not aware of, I repent of it right now. If I have intentionally or unintentionally caused pain to anyone or unjustly offended them, I repent of it right now.

I said: "Lord, if I have any sins of any kind that I have not repented for, I repent of them this very moment." "I now ask Jesus to forgive me of all my sins and cover me in His blood!"

Then all at once, a boldness came over me that I never knew before. And I said these words to Satan: "Devil, I am saved by the blood of Jesus. I am washed in His blood! Jesus' blood is applied to my life!

I have repented of all my sins and they are all now under the blood."

"Devil, I am washed in the blood of Jesus and I right now have a (fresh coat) of blood applied to my heart and life." If you think for one minute that you are big enough to cross over that bloodline to touch me with this restless leg or headaches, then you go right ahead, because I know that you can't cross it, and I challenge you to try right now in Jesus' name!"

I mentioned to Satan that I knew this restless leg syndrome is not of God, and my headaches are not of God, and because of the blood covering Jesus has applied to my life I come against them in the name of Jesus Christ by authority of His name and by the power of His blood!

As of this writing and ever since that night (about fifteen years ago) in my easy chair I have never had one more episode of restless leg syndrome, nor have I had a headache! And, I am not going to have them anymore, because now I know:

How the System Works!

Well, that's my story. And I praise God for the blood. If you are one who doesn't believe Jesus still heals in today's world, I must disagree for personal reasons.

James 5:14-15, "Is any sick among you? Let him call for the elders of the church; and let them pray over him, anointing him with oil in the name of the Lord: **15** And the prayer of faith shall save the sick, and the Lord shall raise him up; and if he have committed sins, they shall be forgiven him."

James (the Lord's brother) said nothing about this authority and power ever leaving the Church upon his death or those of the apostles. It still works because Jesus is the same yesterday, today, and forever! The power of the blood of Jesus still remains! The power of the blood of Jesus has not lost any of its power to save, heal, or to deliver!

God is still the great "I am!" He is not, nor ever will be the great "I was." He does not change, and the blood of Christ does not or has not lost any of its ability, power, or properties.

It seems that today, the church has lost its primary focus, and has gone after the way of Balaam and Cain. Churches are teaching all about prosperity, wealth, personal gain, temporal blessings, luxury vehicles, sixty-five million dollar airplanes, or million dollar homes. Their church sanctuaries now costing in excess of $50 million dollars. The Church now has the attitude: "What can God do for me?" Laodicea is alive and well.

I am not against the blessings of God, but I agree with the old church song: "This world is not my home, I'm just a-passin' through; my treasures are laid up somewhere beyond the blue."

I am sorry, but I think the Church has done everything they can to remove the blood from everything they do. They don't teach it, they no longer sing about it, they don't practice it, and they don't mention it anymore. It seems they would rather teach a works gospel. This is what Jesus said about works:

Mark 14:7, "For ye have the poor with you always, and whensoever ye will ye may do them good: but me ye have not always." It is always a good thing to help the underprivileged whenever we can, but there is no salvation in it.

Once more, I submit to you that if your pastor, church, denomination or movement is preaching something instead of Jesus Christ and Him crucified, or the power of the blood of Jesus, it is most likely preaching a different gospel.

John 8:32, "And ye shall know the truth, and the truth shall make you free. The truth of the gospel and the blood of Jesus Christ, the Son of the living God and only begotten of the Father."

God had respect to Abel's offering because it was a blood sacrifice. As much as the Church wants to run away from the truth of the matter, I can say with all surety that nobody will be saved by another drama team, another fog machine, driving home another

The Gospel According to Job

drunk from the bar, black lights strobe lights and disco balls, passing out some bottled water, some extra Hail Mary's, unbiblically transferring the so-called anointing to someone who may or may not even be saved or worthy of it, helping the proverbial elderly lady cross the street, ecstasis worship, mainlining or tokin' the ghost, another so-called born again movie star celebrity guest speaker, bringing rock and roll and rap music into the Church, another church growth seminar, another so-called prophet's prophecy, some so-called apostle's decree or declaration, someone's new dream or vision, some "new" extra-biblical revelation, warring in the heavenlies, spiritual mapping, completion of the seven mountains mandate, passing through another fire tunnel, learning you are god and can speak whatever you want into existence, somebody's trips to heaven, horoscopes, teaching social justice, the pagan practice of body piercings and tattoo interpretation, some new church programs or curricula, that you are a member of a certain church or denomination, bingo night, a chili supper, or personally being blessed by our Jesuit pope.

If anyone is to receive salvation it will be by the pure unadulterated, God given, unblemished, void of any defects, totally sinless, and sin destroying blood of Jesus Christ that flowed that day like crimson rain down the sides of Calvary's cruel cross! There is no other way! Yes, the old rugged cross made the difference.

Here is a quote from Charles Spurgeon:

"Why should I disbelieve my God? How dare I doubt Him who cannot lie? How can I mistrust the faithful promiser who has added to his promise his oath, and over and above his promise and his oath has given his own blood as a seal?" Charles H. Spurgeon

The blood of Jesus has sealed us. We are sealed, and if sealed, protected by that seal.

To quote William Cowper in his wonderful hymn, "There is a fountain filled with blood drawn from Emmanuel's veins; and sinners plunged beneath that flood lose all their guilty stains." Sadly, most of our churches today don't sing old hymns like this anymore. Seldom will you hear any worship song that even mentions the blood of Jesus or even Jesus by name.

Just as Job was "perfect" in a spiritual way through his keeping his blood covenant and his blood sacrifices, we become perfect through the covering of the blood of Jesus. **2 Corinthians 5:21,** "For He hath made Him *to be* sin for us, who knew no sin; that we might be made the righteousness of God in Him."

That's how the system works!

You do not have to fear that God will just "lift" this protection from you to give Satan access. That is not going to happen. The price paid for your protection is too high! It is too precious for

God to just "lift' it for Satan's advantage. Again, the price is too, too high.

So, repent of your sins and cover yourself in the blood covenant that Jesus made with His own blood. Ask Jesus to be your Lord and Savior. Get your sins under the blood and have them taken away once and for all time.

As a student of Bible prophecy, we can surely see the day approaching, and time is running out. If you are not washed in the blood of Jesus, call on Him today, and you can be. With the removal of the Church, the Antichrist could be on the scene almost immediately. That's how close we are!

Just as God didn't "lift" the hedge of protection from Job, you are secure in the blood of Jesus! Time is running out, now is the day of salvation! Receive Jesus now! Don't delay, the Tribulation is almost upon us, you do not want to be here for it! Jesus is knocking at your heart's door.

Job 42:10, "And the Lord turned the captivity of Job, when he prayed for his friends: also the Lord gave Job twice as much as he had before."

Job 42:12, "So the Lord blessed the latter end of Job more than his beginning: for he had fourteen thousand sheep, and six thousand camels, and a thousand yoke of oxen, and a thousand she asses."

13, "He had also seven sons and three daughters."

Jerry McRaven

Epilogue

In about a week from this writing I am to tape some four television shows with my very close friend and fellow prophecy enthusiast, Miss Susan Turcotte. Susan and I were speakers in a prophecy conference this past summer for two of my good personal friends and local pastors, Gene Coleman and Stan Martin.

One of the topics Susan wants to discuss as the host of her T.V. Program entitled: "The Voice of Rejoicing," is about the subject matter of this book. Perhaps someone will notice or God will direct someone with the wherewithal to get this book published and in the hands of the Body of Christ as my friend, Pastor Monty Roark suggested to me when I began writing it. God knows that I don't know any publishers, and it is doubtful I will try to contact any unless of course God would so direct. If this is truly God's project, it is in His hands now as I have completed my portion. Remember, I never aspired to being an author in the first place.

Speaking of Monty Roark, I remember giving Pastor Monty a copy of Jonathan Cahn's book: The Harbinger. Monty said, "Mac, I have that book already." I suggested to him that he give his book away as a gift and keep the one I gave him since it was a signed copy by Jonathan Cahn.

Later, I gave Monty a copy of Chuck Missler's book: "Hidden Treasures in the Bible Text." Brother Monty told me he had that book also. I again suggested Monty give his book away as a gift and keep mine as Chuck Missler had signed it.

Finally, I gave Monty a copy of Bill Koenig's book: "Eye to Eye." Once more Monty said, "But Mac, I have this book already." Again I could only suggest one last time, "Just give your copy away as a gift to someone and keep the one I gave you as it is signed by Bill Koenig. "

Monty then said, "Hey Mac, be sure to write the book about "How the System Works." The Body of Christ needs it. Oh, by the way Mac, I want a signed copy."

I said, "Monty, you got that coming."

ABOUT THE AUTHOR

Jerry McRaven, or Brother "MAC" as he is known to his friends, is a 4th generation Full Gospel Minister. He began his ministry as a youth Evangelist and has also pastored. Brother Mac spent twenty-five years working in the Missouri State Prison System in different capacities, but ultimately spending twenty years as a Recreation Officer or "Coach Mac" as the inmate residents knew him. Brother Mac served for many years in a supervisory capacity in the Recreation Department where this placement was a perfect opportunity to mentor and counsel the inmate residents and to steer them in the right godly direction. Brother McRaven would also speak at the two inmate Chapels at the institution.

Earlier in his career, Brother Mac spent 7 years in the U.S. Navy as a Hospital Corpsman and functioned as a Licensed EMT and a Field Medical Service Technician with the U.S. Marines. As a result of his military service, Brother McRaven has traveled extensively and has witnessed first-hand the many cultures and religious ideologies in the world and has noticed their impact in world affairs. Brother McRaven is an avid student of Bible Prophecy and attends Prophecy Conferences and Summits whenever his schedule allows. From his many years of research, Brother McRaven believes we are living in the very end of time, and the Return of Christ for His Church is imminent.

Jerry McRaven

Brother McRaven has been married to his wife, Janice for over thirty-three years and they have one son, Joshua McRaven. Mac and Janice are available as "Full-Time" Evangelists and Camp Meeting or Conference Speakers. If you have an event or would just like to schedule Brother McRaven, you can contact him by email: jerrymcraven@yahoo.com.

BIBLIOGRAPHY

BIBLES

Dakes Annotated Reference Bible, (pgs. 64 & 65; 96), Dake Publishing Inc., Large Print Ed. (Nov.,2010).

Grant Jeffrey Study Bible, Nothing Directly used, except referenced this Bible when researching the sermon, "How the System Works."

The Holy Bible New International Version (NIV Bible), Hawes Publications, (Online) Publications last update: (Sept. 30, 2015). Quoted: The NIV says it this way: "For the secret power of lawlessness is already at work; but the one who now holds it back will continue to do so till he is taken out of the way."

J.P. Green Interlinear Bible, Nothing Directly used, except referenced this Bible when researching the sermon: "How the System Works."

New American Standard Bible (NASB), www.biblestudytools.com/nas, p. 134, quoted: "For the mystery of lawlessness is already at work; only He who now restrains *will do so* until He is taken out of the way."

REFERENCE MATERIALS/QUOTES

Hale, Leslie, (The Irish Preacher), p. 66, Received this teaching from Leslie Hale: Because of Psalm 22, and many other scriptures, Satan had over 1000 years to keep Jesus from going to the cross, but he was not able to stop Jesus from fulfilling prophecy. (Teaching from Leslie Hale Ministries, P.O. Box 125, Tarpon Springs, Fl. 34688 (www.LeslieHale.com), (Time and Date Unknown).

"LDS Church News Week," Hinckley, Gordon B. quote, "In bearing testimony of Jesus Christ, . . ." spoken by the late Mormon

Jerry McRaven

Prophet, Deseret News, Church News Section, Salt Lake City, Utah, Week ending (June 20th, 1998) p. 7.

II Maccabees 5:11-14, USCCB.org, United States Conference of Catholic Bishops translation of II Maccabees (Online), p. 114

Wikipedia, https://www.wikipedia.org/ (Nothing directly used, except I used this website for general information when researching the sermon: "How the System Works.")

Wikipedia, https://www.wikipedia.org/ ,"We also are aware that the fetus or infant child in the mother's womb does not come into direct contact with the blood of the mother." (p.63). Wikipedia: Fetal Circulation (June 2011) (Online).

AUTHORS

Brumley, Albert E., Quote: "This world is not my home, I'm just a-passin'through; my treasures are laid up somewhere beyond the blue." Copyright (1937 Renewed 1965), Albert E. Brumley & Sons, Hymnary.org. p 151.

Cowper, William, Song, "There is a Fountain Filled With Blood," Published (1772), Copyright (Public Domain), Timeless Truths Free Online Library, verse quoted on the p. 153.

Jones, Lewis, Song, "Power in the Blood" Copyright Public Domain, Timeless Truths Free Online Library, p.103, (1899).

Spurgeon, Charles H., Sermon #1033, "Faith's Dawn and It's Clouds," Delivered (Jan. 28th 1872). p. 153, quoted on the page.

Various Websites for General Information
Nothing directly used, except such were used in researching for the Sermon: "How the System Works."

"How the System Works"

Sermon by: Jerry McRaven (Book Based upon this Sermon by Author) (1999).

Jerry McRaven

www.ingramcontent.com/pod-product-compliance
Lightning Source LLC
Chambersburg PA
CBHW061948070426
42450CB00007BA/1093